TOM JACKSON

He is one of the nation's top manpower and employment experts. His experience is with corporations, schools and government agencies.

Jackson is responsible for the design of many skills and manpower matching programs, job development and placement systems, and outplacement facilities for terminated employees.

Over three hundred top employers now use his successful *New Dimensions in Employment Interviewing* to train their personnel in hiring techniques. He is the acclaimed author of *The Hidden Job Market,* published by The New York Times; *28 Days to a Better Job,* published by Hawthorn. His "The Job Game" is used by schools, corporations, and community groups across the country.

In *Guerrilla Tactics in the Job Market* he tells you where the hot growth areas will be in the 1980s, and specific tactics to help you get the kind of work which will provide personal satisfaction and a good paycheck.

Bantam Books of Related Interest
Ask your bookseller for the books you have missed

THE BUSINESS WRITING HANDBOOK
  by William C. Paxson
EVERYTHING A WOMAN NEEDS TO KNOW TO
  GET PAID WHAT SHE'S WORTH
  by Caroline Bird
THE GAMESMAN by Michael Maccoby
GUERRILLA TACTICS IN THE JOB MARKET
  by Tom Jackson
MANAGEMENT AND MACHIAVELLI
  by Anthony Jay
MARKETING YOURSELF: The Catalyst Women's
  Guide to Successful Resumes and Interviews
  by The Catalyst Staff
NO-NONSENSE MANAGEMENT
  by Richard S. Sloma
YOU CAN NEGOTIATE ANYTHING
  by Herb Cohen

GUERRILLA TACTICS IN THE JOB MARKET

BY TOM JACKSON

BANTAM BOOKS
TORONTO · NEW YORK · LONDON · SYDNEY

GUERRILLA TACTICS IN THE JOB MARKET
A Bantam Book / August 1978
2nd printing .... January 1979
3rd printing .... July 1980
4th printing ... September 1981

All rights reserved.
Copyright © 1978 by Tom Jackson.
This book may not be reproduced in whole or in part, by mimeograph or any other means, without permission.
For information address: Bantam Books, Inc.

ISBN 0-553-20599-4

Published simultaneously in the United States and Canada

Bantam Books are published by Bantam Books, Inc. Its trademark, consisting of the words "Bantam Books" and the portrayal of a rooster is Registered in U.S. Patent and Trademark Office and in other countries. Marca Registrada. Bantam Books, Inc., 666 Fifth Avenue, New York, New York 10103.

PRINTED IN THE UNITED STATES OF AMERICA

ACKNOWLEDGMENT

There are people in my life who make a difference. They have created this book with me, and through me. Heidi Sparkes is a warrior who won't ever take the easy way out—always through. Lynn Stiles is articulate and clear where I am dumb. Ron Bynum has gifted me with his outrageousness and compassion. Louise Jones keeps my life in order and stands behind me. Patti Fox, Bill Williams, and Lynn Krown are workers who create their own jobs daily out of love and support. And Ellen, of course, is the music to my words.

This book is from all of us.

HAVE IT YOUR WAY

To Dave —

Best of luck in
the cruel job world.
From one who's experienced
mixed success

Joe

CONTENTS

1. WORKLIFE: YOUR NEXT TEN THOUSAND DAYS ... 1

2. WHO ARE YOU, AND WHAT ARE YOU GOING TO DO ABOUT IT? ... 23

3. JOBS FOR THE '80S AND BEYOND ... 47

4. TARGETING ... 71

5. WORK EDUCATION ... 99

6. INSIDE THE HIDDEN JOB MARKET ... 109

7. THE UNIVERSAL HIRING RULE ... 155

8. THE WAY IN ... 187

9. THE DIRECTED INTERVIEW ... 235

10. END GAME ... 263

INTRODUCTION

Gentle Reader:

This book is designed to awaken in you a new sense of how to get what you want from the part of your life which you see as your worklife. It is written with the understanding that most people pretty much take for granted the enormous amount of time which they spend either on a job, or trying to get a job or wishing that they had the right kind of work. It comes out of the recognition that most of us rarely get the opportunity to experience our own power in identifying and locating work opportunities which feed us in a deeper way than with a paycheck.

The information abstractions and observations of how the workworld is structured come from the author's direct experience over the past 15 years with thousands of job seekers, employer representatives, career consultants, philosophers, authors, and other authorities engaged indirectly or directly with man's relation to the workworld. We have tried to examine and digest everything valuable in this area, and to incorporate whatever could make a contribution.

Besides observations and principles related to the work experience we have provided the reader with a set of action-based tactics which can be used to actually produce specific results in the search for increased work satisfaction or a better job. These tactics arise out of the pragmatic experience of our work with real individuals confronting the real world of the job search. They have been proved to be effective in actual case by case experience. By following the tactics, the reader will be able to obtain for himself the kinds of results and benefits promised in the text. The tactics frequently require a confrontation and a lot of work and participation. There is no easier way to get what you want.

This book deals with the contexts of the work experience—the underlying principles which are rarely discussed or revealed. It is by understanding and experiencing this foundation and applying the tactics that the reader will be able to generate his own experience and success in his worklife, and to free himself forever from the idea that there is a scarcity of opportunity and personal aliveness in the work experience.

Much of the underlying space or context from which this book has been generated is the result of the author's experience with Werner Erhard, the source of the *est* training and organization, to whom the book is lovingly dedicated.

> Tom Jackson
> New York City
> November 1977

1

WORKLIFE: YOUR NEXT TEN THOUSAND DAYS

HELLO

We are here to bring you some good news about your life.

The purpose of this book is to put you in touch with an increased ability to experience satisfaction in the day-to-day pursuit of your worklife. To expand your ability to get in touch with who you are, and to use the virtually universal experience of work as an opportunity to produce value for others, and increased aliveness for yourself.

And we know that as you tentatively absorb these initial words, you may doubt what we say. You've heard it before. You're bored with unkept promises, and probably skeptical that any book can ultimately make a major contribution to your life.

We understand your skepticism. It is hard to believe that there is much to say about a subject which has been knocking around for so many millennia. What is there to learn about work? You do your best, find a job that's not so bad, and try to make the most of it. Yes, you try to make the most of it.

The bad news is that something like 80% of the people in this nation (and world) spend the ten thousand days of their working life at jobs about which they have had very little choice, and which they do not experience as nurturing and exciting. It has become commonplace to assume that the work experience is something one puts up with, a necessary evil, a social duty. Take a slice through the workforce and ask five people about their work experience, and you will find two people who will clearly tell you that they don't like their jobs, another two who are not satisfied but do not admit it publicly, and *one* person who relishes the work experience with exuberance and joie de vivre and doesn't mind telling you so. Don't take our word for it, just park yourself outside an office building or factory at quitting time. Or, better yet, monitor the conversations of men and women returning home from their hard day's work: If you do, you will learn fatigue, boredom, anger, jealousy, frustration, stress, resentment, and regret. Grievances. If one thing is clear about the contemporary American work experience, it is that there is not much joy or aliveness in it for many of us. Living is reserved for after 5:00 p.m., and on weekends.

The further good news is that it's no longer necessary to dramatize the same old soap opera. It's no longer obligatory to accept the next job which comes along in the career field you find yourself in after school. The New American Job Game is on, and you are a player. The new game, which you may have started to hear about only in the last year or so, starts with the proposition that the work experience is the primary human/social/economic relationship, and that the quality of one's work experience directly influences or controls the quality of one's life experience. Your work and your life are inseparably related. Worklife/lifework.

This book is a player's manual for the new game. It comes out of 15 years of direct on-line experience with secretaries, executives, managers, college kids, adventurers, entrepreneurs, carpenters, construction workers, sailors, intellectuals, women, blacks, employers, placement and guidance counselors, and dozens of other authors, lecturers, and authorities in the growing field of career and life planning.

Our objective is to reveal to you not just the how to, the strategies and tactics of the career/life search, but also the contexts and abstractions from which they spring. The underlying principles which have been realized during hundreds of workshops and thousands of hours of direct pragmatic exposure to the work reality.

What we want you to get is an expanded, more creative view of the game. To see your worklife as an opportunity to play, and in the playing to experience true aliveness and satisfaction. To be alive and working at the same time.

TACTICS

So that you can move beyond the abstractions into a more direct and practical application of your own career/life search, we have included a numbered set of specific tactics developed from actual workshop experiences, which you can use to put the material to work for yourself. You may want to follow these exercises and action steps as you proceed, or to go through the book just reading the material, and come back and make a second pass doing all the tactics in order. Either way, if you organize a notebook in advance, and use it to record and work out the assignments, you will add a level of practicality to the book which will support you in recognizing and obtaining the work targets which will get you what you want in your life.

Norm Blessing

When Norm Blessing started work down at the plant he knew that it would only be for a few months—until he got everything straightened out. Once he got some bread together and had a chance to sit down and sort out what he really wanted to do with his life, then he would go out and get a better job, something with more responsibility, more money. As he put it: "This factory work is for yo-yos, people without much ambition. But it's a good place to get a fat paycheck without working too hard. The kind of job I really want will be in business—something like my brother, Walt. But right now I've got to handle these bills. In two or three months I'm gonna make my move. This baby's gonna surprise you."

That was 12 years ago. Here's how his wife, Maggie, describes the experience now:

> Norm was always an optimist. The unbelievable thing is that he still is. He talks about changing jobs every few months. I love his hope and enthusiasm, but inside, it makes me sad. He doesn't really like his job. He won't complain about it much but it shows. I see it. He feels that there are others things he could be doing, something with wood or building—he's

really incredible with his hands—but he hasn't been able to turn up anything. A few years ago he took a month off to see if he could get work as a carpenter, but it didn't work. It is complicated to break into the union around here, and he really doesn't want to build houses.

The thing is that I know he could do real well in another field, one that he would enjoy. But how do you find it? It's a mystery to me how people get good jobs. It's not just education—you read about those college graduates driving cabs—it's knowing where to go, what to say, who to see.

Norm Blessing is still at the plant, dreaming of a day when he will be happy to go to work in the morning— in a job which pays him more than a paycheck. He has put in 3000 days at jobs he doesn't like. He has 7000 workdays left in his life, and he could use them in a way which guarantees built-in satisfaction—and not just on payday. But he doesn't know how to go about it.

Trish David

Trish's school years were a great adventure for her. Her bachelor uncle Bill had, much to everyone's surprise and her delight, agreed to pay her tuition to any school she wanted to go to if she and the family would meet the other expenses, which they could just manage. Trish picked Bryn Mawr College on Philadelphia's posh Main Line. Her mother and father put up a fuss when she chose such an expensive school, but with the easy acquiescence of Uncle Bill, her excellent grades, and an agreement that Trish would work summers, she had her way, and packed herself off to the upper crust while most of her high-school friends headed for Penn State.

One of Trish's hobbies was dressmaking. At home she had always made clothes for her mother and older sister, and she picked up spending money by doing costumes for the local theater group and dresses for her friends at school. This skill paid big dividends. Not only did she make all her own things, she also made simple, but interesting and attractive shirts and dresses which she sold to campus friends. During the first two summers she worked as an assistant designer at a custom dress shop near her home.

Disaster struck in the middle of her second summer. Just as Trish was starting to plan for the upcoming junior year, Uncle Bill lost everything in a Wall Street failure, and Trish was told that she couldn't return to school. She was stopped cold. It was a major shock, and Trish lost her enthusiasm and resourcefulness, quit her job, and for two months barely left her room. Eventually she took a job in her sister's firm, a travel agency specializing in Bahamas and Caribbean vacations. She became an agent, and although the work didn't really turn her on, was able to get by and earn a reasonable salary. She stopped making her own clothes, and that part of her life seemed to be a thing of the past.

In a couple of years, Trish married a successful New York businessman, and some of the old style returned: expensive restaurants, travel, plays, and the fringes of the jet set.

After spending three fast-paced years in New York, Trish moved to Fort Lauderdale, where her husband was a partner in a large condominium project. The pace slowed. Trish says:

> Florida life was really easy. Perfect weather, and lots of tennis. But it was boring after New York. After two months I had had enough pina colada lunches to last a lifetime, and I decided to put my work act back together. I hadn't been employed for three years, and I had an urge to do something productive. Naturally, I went back to clothes, my first love.
>
> I started by making some new things for myself. The tennis dress was a big hit. It was rather a challenge to do something original, since at that time a tennis dress was a tennis dress was a tennis dress. But my sexy new model caught on and I started making them for my friends. Soon everyone had to have one, and I was faced with a decision: either give it up—my joints were stiff from making them myself—or find someone to help, and make them commercially. My achievement instincts were

aroused again. What I really wanted to do was to get back to work, and to connect it with my love of clothes and designing.

Trish personally contacted every garment manufacturer between Miami and Orlando. And, eventually, she created a job at a fashionable chain of boutiques with stores in Miami, Palm Beach, New York, and Chicago. We say "created" because when she first appeared they turned her down. They had just hired someone. She returned a week later with a set of sketches for some unusual tennis dresses which she felt would be perfect for their fancy clientele. She was right, and got the job she wanted. Trish is now a very well-paid designer with a successful garment manufacturer, and has regained all her old spirit and confidence. She knows that the key ingredient in a successful life is having a job which lets you be who you are.

THE HIGH COST OF EARNING A LIVING

The average worklife is about ten thousand days long: more time than people devote to any other activity in their lives. It is a big number to begin with, but when you stop to realize that work takes up the prime years of your life (after schooling, and before retirement) and the prime hours of the day, you will begin to get the picture:

For all intents and purposes your work is your life. The message from shrinks, counselors, correction officials, and others in the combat zone of our society is quite clear:

The degree of satisfaction which you get from your work directly affects the degree of health and vitality in the rest of your life.

If you settle for work which just pays the bills, which has as its cost hours of boredom and dissatisfaction, you will find that you are paying for your job in human terms at a cost which far exceeds the take-home pay.

This is true at all levels of work. A corner office with a window, a carpet on the floor, and a title on the door is no insurance against the deadness of work which does not represent who you are. The "martini manager" is a social type which attests to this. All his life he has worked for and dreamed about becoming a manager. Now he is one, and it takes twice-daily doses of martinis on the rocks for him to handle the pain and disappointment when he discovers that the name on the door hasn't changed anything. More money and a title is only more money and a title. It has nothing to do with satisfaction. Please know that. It is observably true.

Just "working for a living" is unfortunately one of the least assailable things to do in life. It is approved by church, state, schools, parents, children, the Department of Labor, guidance counselors, your older brother, the next-door neighbors, and your friends. It is natural. A logical step in the child-school-work-marriage-children-more work-retirement-death scenario that all of us are very familiar with. "Get a job" is the familiar battle cry from contented capitalists and striving socialists to comradely communists.

> Get a job!
> "Where?" you say.
> It doesn't matter, stay close to home.
> "But doing *what*?"
> Whatever you've been trained for.
> "I don't think there are any jobs in that field."
> Well, don't worry about that, get *something*, start at the bottom, work your way up.
> "To what?"
> To the top.
> "I want to find something I like."
> Like? Who said working had anything to do with liking it!

Stress kills as many people as war. Work you don't like is close to the top of the list of stress generators. Not having a job produces even more stress than having a job you don't like, and that is part of the problem. People who are entering the job market for the first time, with little or no tools to aid them, and with almost no idea of how to proceed intelligently, really feel under pressure to get a job—any job—and the longer it takes the worse most people feel. It gets very lonely when your friends are away at work and you're sitting around trying to figure out the system. You start to wonder what's wrong, why me? After a few weeks with no direction, little or no guidance, and feeling more and more like a loser, almost everyone succumbs to the next acceptable job which comes along.

> "Hi, Helen—how's the new work?"
> "Oh, not so bad" (hating it), "it's a job."
> Short-term gain, lifetime loss.

TACTIC #1

Get yourself a large notebook to use as you go through this book. Even if you plan to come back and do the exercises later, get the notebook now so you are prepared when the mood strikes you. Note the number of each tactic when you do it.

List everything you can think of about work which you don't like. You can list general things, or aspects of specific jobs you have held.

When you've done that, list everything you know or can think of which you like, or feel you could like about the work experience.

COMPLETION CHECK ☐

THE NEW WORK REVOLUTION

You are in the middle of an opportunity revolution, but we know it doesn't always look like it.

At the time this book is being put together, there are three or four million *brand-new* jobs being added to the labor force each year. This year. That comes down to over 65,000 brand new jobs each week. This week. An expanding job market. And we're not ignoring the unemployment rate of between 6% and 7%, which is largely a result of the great expansion of the workforce. More jobs, and more workers. If you're stuck on the bad news we'll let you have 7% unemployment to complain about. (And more than double that if you are black.) But we want you to be willing to look at the other side of the bad news. If 7% (or 14%) of the workforce is out of work, what is the *em*ployment rate? Yes, a whopping 93% (or 86%). Not bad odds. As a matter of fact, how many games do you get to play where the odds are in your favor so dramatically?

Digression (skip this if you aren't interested in the big picture):

The fear that takes hold with rising unemployment is very contagious, and often self-fulfilling.

The New York Times *breaks the story: "Unemployment UP—Millions Looking for Work."*

Bud Colleger, riding to work from his estate in Greenwich, Connecticut, makes a mental note that things are going downhill, and to hold back that new order of 10,000 barbecue units until things turn around a bit.

Lynn Cohen gets serious when she sees it, and decides not to hire those two new production assistants. Who knows, there might be some cutbacks coming.

Jean and Harry Altshuler have a family meeting. Perhaps this is not the best time to ask for a two-month sabbatical—let's hold off.

And Dan Christopher looks satisfied. Misery loves company. He knew it was coming. Now he's got the perfect reason for being out of work. It's hopeless! "Millions are looking—how can I get something in this market?"

Unemployment is not a disease which rises out of the cranberry bogs and wafts across the land like pollution. It is not a cause of anything. Unemployment is a reflection of a society in transition. There is certainly no shortage of jobs to be done in this and several future lifetimes. Unemployment is simply the measure of imbalance between what tasks need to be done in a society and the time it takes to recognize them and mobilize the workforce.

In 1973 the oil shortage that everyone had been predicting for decades finally showed up. Surprise! Within

WORKLIFE: YOUR NEXT TEN THOUSAND DAYS 11

six months Detroit discovers the small car. Naturally, the first thing that happens is that big-car plants close down and thousands are laid off in related lines while everyone figures how to get next year's small cars out of the factories, and this year's big cars out of the lots. So while management discusses, and plans and budgets, thousands of workers associated in some way with gas guzzlers cool their heels.

When plans are made, budgets are put to bed, and capital is released from bank vaults, Ford and Chevy start to hire again, and unemployment insurance clerks start to worry about their jobs.

There is not a piece of legislation, environmental crisis, or major weather pattern change which doesn't affect the job market, which responds to the degree that forces are aligned behind new directions, new solutions, new ways to create something. We say it again: In national terms, unemployment doesn't cause anything (other than the late night news jitters). It measures.

The rate of unemployment is the measure of the society's inability to come up with solutions.

It is also a measure of the individual's inability to be in touch with his own skills, and translate them effectively. Yes, the individual creates unemployment to the degree that he or she is stuck at the kitchen table not knowing his or her own abilities, or where to plug them in.

End of digression. As we were saying, one aspect of the work revolution is the large number of new jobs being created each week. A great growth opportunity. Another major factor in today's workworld is the incredible variety of new things that need to be done. The types of problems which need to be solved are expanding even faster than the number of new jobs being added.

According to people who watch these things (Bucky Fuller, Alvin Toffler, and others), we are at a point in the development of human potential where the curve is just about leaving the chart. We are no longer accurately in a growth period. We are in an explosion. As we move through an age of superindustrialization, we are experiencing a degree of technology and work change which seemed impossible and far-fetched a generation ago, and still seems unbelievable to most. As Toffler put it in his brilliant book *Future Shock*: "We are creating a new society. Not a changed society. Not an extended, larger-than-life version of our present society. But a new society."

It is ultrasafe to say that there is now five times the diversity in jobs that there was a decade ago. And the game is still expanding faster than anyone can keep up with it. Virtually every field from agriculture to zoology has had its neatly organized workcharts knocked over like a house of cards in a squall. So fast does the change come that even the experts in the affected fields are hard put to describe what's happening.

Opportunity is exploding, that's what's happening. And you are the beneficiary. What the work revolution means is that new opportunities to deal with and solve local, national, and planetary problems are there for the asking. There is enough variety now for people to virtually design the game they want to play. All they need is the system.

TACTIC #2

In your newly started workbook, list ten problems—large or small—which exist in the world today. These can be problems or needs which show up in your home town, country, continent, planet, or universe. Keep them real—things which you have seen with your own eyes. (Examples: Streets need to be better marked, a local manufacturer needs better hiring practices, people need more consumer product information, someone needs to develop a new day-care center, an office needs to be organized.)

COMPLETION CHECK [ ]

A SYSTEM TO BEAT THE SYSTEM

How much did your education cost? Do you know? With variations (plus or minus 20%) this is what was shelled out by you, your family, your government, or other philanthropists, to get you through school.

IF YOU STOPPED AT—	YOUR EDUCATION COST—
2 years high school	$10,700
4 years high school	$11,913
2 years college	$16,637
4 years private college	$21,523
4 years public college	$18,016
Master's Degree	$24,378
Ph.D.	$26,852
Lawyer	$36,628
M.D.	$75,000

Wherever you got off, it cost a small fortune to get you there. Education is the largest social investment. It has a potential for elevating men's vision beyond almost anything imagined.

We have learned how to read and write, how to build, how to destroy, how to calculate, how to run multi-million-dollar machines, and how to locate a fading star, create stage productions to delight kings and queens, mend a broken heart, sew up a ruptured kidney, speak to dolphins, make music, and govern entire continents. We left one thing out:

How to find work which we enjoy and which nurtures us.

This is equivalent to spending ten years building an immense space probe, and leaving out the delivery system.

In visits to over a hundred major two- and four-year campuses, meeting students on their way out to the real world, we see that perhaps one in four has an idea of a valid job target for him- or herself. Less than one in ten is clear about the relationship of work to personal goals and purposes. Not many know what they have to offer to a potential employer. Almost none has a comprehensive job search plan. All payload, and no delivery system.

If the choice were available, which it isn't, I would recommend a three-month intensive course in how to deal effectively with the workworld in place of a master's thesis.

Once you know the basics of the delivery system—personal appraisal, targeting, identifying opportunity, communicating value, job finding, getting paid for delivering benefit, dealing with change, and identifying resources—you are in an excellent position to locate the kinds of jobs which will work for you, and produce a direct ongoing experience of pleasure and satisfaction.

One thing becomes more and more clear through work with thousands of applicants and hundreds of employers: *It's not the most qualified persons who get the best jobs, it's those who are most skilled in job finding.* That's why this book was written: to get you in touch with a system to beat the system.

SUCCESS

Drake Vaughan

I took my first job right out of the navy when I returned to Seattle from San Diego. A good job, too. I had wanted something associated with transportation. But mostly, what I wanted was to "make it," whatever that means. What it meant for me then was simple: a fatter paycheck every month. No frills, no psychic rewards, just a few extra numbers and I'd be happy. I started at $9500 per year as assistant dispatcher at a trucking firm. That wasn't too bad in those days. In about six months though, I had set my life up so that I was spending pretty much everything I earned on payments. Really, I would end up with about $20 per week for extras.

What I had to do was very simple; I had to make more money. No problem. Shined my shoes, bought a nice vest, and I turned to that goal. By the end of my first year I got a raise, and a promotion. They pushed my pay up to $12,000 per year. After taxes that came to around ten grand. It sounds solid,

WORKLIFE: YOUR NEXT TEN THOUSAND DAYS

doesn't it? Ten grand. It took me about three weeks to absorb the difference. A new MG to replace my old Ford. That was about it.

The next step was $15,000—which gave me a clear $1000 and change each month. I was really elated—my progession seemed assured. Well, not exactly elated, I guess, the job was getting to be a bitch to handle: more responsibility, more trucks to dispatch, and two assistants to do most of the paperwork. You've never seen more paperwork anywhere. I really didn't like the job then, and if the truth be known, I don't much care for the field now. It's too frantic, always hustling.

Anyway, I stuck it out, and continued up the ladder. Salary jumps to $25,000 were easy, and then things started to level. The raises were smaller, on a percentage basis. I was close to the top. A big frog in a small pond. But an aggressive one. I had married by then and we bought a house. It's crazy, isn't it, every time you start to put aside some cash something comes along that you've just got to do. A trip, a house, a kid, another kid. I was damn near broke making $27,500 when I decided to take a new job down in Portland.

This guy had been after me for years to take over and run his interstate trucking business. I had resisted, since I really loved it in Seattle. Anyway, we went to Portland for more money. How much more? Well, it was a base of $30,000 plus some profit sharing promised. I loved it for a while. Here I was ten years in trucking, 37 years old, earning over $30,000. A great wife and two kids now. And success. I was running my own show. It sounds good, doesn't it?

There were a few dark clouds, however. First of all, the feeling of success tarnished like cheap brass plate. The game got stale. It wasn't that bad as jobs go, but it got boring after I'd solved the same problems a few hundred times over. And we are still broke. I mean if I were to lose this job now I don't know how we'd manage. We have virtually no savings. It's funny, but after we pay all our bills and taxes, guess what we have at the end of each week to do what we want with—about $20!

What is success? Cash in the bank? A secure job, a title, status? Perhaps all of it? Watch out, danger ahead. Success contains a trap which has pinned many a good player. The trap is this: *There is never enough.* When you're making $10,000 it looks like the people at $15,000 are really successful. When you're at $15,000 per year it looks like at $25,000 you would really be in good shape. Success, for most, is something out there, something to go after. And it can never be possessed. It's always just around the corner.

It's fine if you are successful. Just don't sell out your personal day-to-day work satisfaction to get it. As far as we can see, there is very little inherent satisfaction in chasing success just to be successful. For sure there is never enough money. You can play that game for three decades and not come out on top. Money still doesn't buy happiness. And of course neither does poverty. You've heard it, and you don't believe it. That's OK. We want you to play the game fully. Make more money. Have more fun. Be successful!

But do it within a day-to-day framework that satisfies you. *Real success is having a job that works for you.* When you get connected to work you like *in and of itself*, that reflects who you are, allows you to express yourself, you can't lose.

Ed Winn

I don't believe that I get paid to do this. I love to fly. I would gladly pay to do it. And I get paid for it! Of course, being a company pilot has its bad side, at least you could make it seem bad. Lots of waiting, some down time tearing apart a faulty magneto. Greasy. But you should know that I used to rush home from school to do this without pay, so it's not a problem.

And these guys I fly around. Incredible. Three lawyers from Atlanta who handle cases all around the South. One day in Baton Rouge, two days in Raleigh. Sometimes I just hang out with them in a city rather than crank it up and head home. They are fabulous to watch in court. I've even been toying with the idea of going to law school. They're just crazy enough to let me do it. As I said, I've got a great job. The pay is secondary.

Joy Watkins

I would get into a plane if it was very important. And I do, once or twice a year. White-knuckle flight. This programming job requires very little travel and that's the way I want it.

And the real reason I'm here is that I like to work by myself. You can do that in programming. It's a long series of elegant puzzles. Well, that's rather poetic, some of them aren't so elegant. But I still get a charge when I rack it in for the third time and it lights up. The system works. There is no doubt when it works that I was responsible. That's when I like being with people. When I demonstrate their new system and they see a machine do what it had taken them so long to do by hand. That's fun. They don't understand the first thing about what I do. They just look at the printouts and look at me and shake their heads in disbelief. I love it. The pay is OK, probably below average. But what a big toy they give you to play with.

REAL SUCCESS IS HAVING A JOB WHICH LETS YOU PLAY

TACTIC #3

List three work-related tasks or activities which you really love to do—would pay to do if necessary.

Now think of at least two real-life paying jobs which feature the two activities. Stretch your thinking if you need to.

COMPLETION CHECK

WORKING PAPERS—THE COLLEGE DEGREE

According to *College Graduates and Their Employers*, Report No. 4, published in 1975 by the CPC Foundation: "By 1971 barely more than half the graduates were employed in the occupations they planned to enter in 1965."

It is common knowledge that for some areas of study (such as history, philosophy, and fine arts) there are virtually no directly relevant positions for most graduates. The slowness with which the education establishment expands to the changing needs of society is an example of one of the more highly entrenched bureaucracies keeping itself going.

The debate is long and clamorous: "Education should remain pure—untouched by the needs of the marketplace" on the one hand, and "We need to prepare students for business" on the other. We won't get caught in the academic cross fire except to suggest that there is probably room for both. Students definitely should be schooled in the rich tapestry of the humanities and the arts; everyone should have the opportunity to expand their vision beyond commercial needs. On the other hand, it is a rip-off to put an individual youngster through an incredibly expensive, lengthy, privileged education, and not ground him in ways he can *use his* learning in the world not only to expand his own growth and participation, but to contribute to others.

The employment manager of one of the nation's largest recruiters of college talent says this: "We have an earnest and real desire to bring people across a wide range of disciplines into our management training programs. We think it adds to our own depth. But sometimes it's hopeless. So many of your history and philosophy majors know virtually nothing about business. We sometimes just look across the desk at each other and shrug our shoulders. Kids should be given more insight into what jobs are, where they are, how to present themselves."

Employers look for education; then they squander it. A low-level administrative post requires a four-year degree. Some secretarial positions want at least two years of college. Part of this is a kind of snobbism: "We use only the best raw materials." Another reason is the simple fact that by making it into school, and completing it, you proved something about yourself. It simplifies the hiring process. Of course, it also discriminates heavily against people who didn't make it in, couldn't get the small legacy together, or have been branded with a lousy high-school record. Unfair? Yes, but that's the way it is. If you can get together a college degree—two years are OK, four are preferred—do so, even if you are a dozen years behind. You will be paid back lavishly in higher earning potential, increased mobility, and more interesting jobs. It is a kind of passport.

SORRY—NO PASSPORT

If you don't have a college education, you still have the potential to confront the job world and uncover rewarding and satisfying work choices, and even to be one of the large tribe of folk heroes who "made it up the hard way." But for you, it is absolutely essential to get a good understanding of how the job market delivery system works. We're not writing you off, we're writing you in.

There are hundreds of programs of noncollege-degree education available, ranging from trade and vocational schools to adult education and apprenticeship programs. You can be trained to be a gourmet chef or a bush pilot if you are willing to put yourself out. This is discussed in greater detail in chapter five.

ONE WORKLIFE—FOUR CAREERS

Work has a bad name. It is confused with its second-level meaning involving energy, ergs, and effort.

When *we* write about work we are talking about what you do in relationship to society. It's your game, your role, your contribution. When you boil it down, you get to see two primary human relationships: love and work.

And just as you will have different loves in your life, you will have several different careers.

It used to be that people would "enter a career" with almost a family feeling: "Dad spent his years here, and now I'm coming aboard." It wasn't too long ago that if you worked in banking at the middle management level, for example, you would find it virtually impossible to join a competitive bank in the same city. Many industries were the same. Loyalty to the employees, loyalty back to the employer. Job changes occurred twice or at most three times in an entire professional career. Today the average job duration has shrunk. White-collar unions and organized technical/management communications have strengthened the power of people to change jobs, and carry their expertise with them to another post.

It started with employers' needs to bring in new technologies and methods, as managers in our information-oriented business system found they couldn't keep up without stepping out of their own body of knowledge. This was dramatized in the early and mid-'60s when the big space race was on, and McDonnell Douglas, North American Aviation, Lockheed, and Boeing were buying up as many engineers as they could find. A new graduate electrical engineer could have six to ten offers of employment, several from firms that he had never visited.

At the end of the decade the adventure wound down, and tens of thousands of aerospace technologists were unceremoniously dumped onto the job market. It was raw: $15,000 to $25,000-a-year engineers would report to work on a Monday morning to find their entire floor cleared out, all their personal goods in a box, with a pink slip entitling them to a month's severance. Easy come, easy go.

Today the musical chairs is less obvious, but firms in fast-growing technical fields such as oceanography, videogames, microelectronics, and network TV can't make it without a steady infusion of new talents and new ideas. An official at Western Union, for example, guessed that probably 80% of the jobs they now have didn't exist a dozen years ago. Telegrams have gone out of style.

Management has caught the bug, too. Top-level

changes are now the rule rather than the exception. Executives with a track record can virtually write their own first-class ticket. Jumps across entire industries are not uncommon.

Geographic change is also much more frequent these days. One out of five families moves each year: some in response to mergers and acquisitions, or corporate relocation, others just to experience a new place to live. It's not necessary to be as rooted anymore. If you don't like Montana winters, move to Miami, or Houston, or San Diego. A major factor in your job choice can and probably should be where you want to live.

Given the feverish rate of technical obsolescence, new products, new battles in the war for some environmental sanity, new consumer demands, social legislation, the youth movement, the senior citizen movement, the singles movement, the gay movement, the women's movement, and your own developing ideas of who you are, it is inevitable that you will have not only up to ten job changes in your lifetime, but perhaps three or four complete changes in career path:

From stockbroker to go-go dancer
From actress to media planner
From minister to career counselor
From secretary to programmer
From housewife to lawyer
From construction worker to landscape gardener
From corporate executive to yacht captain
From bottle washer to cook
From advertising executive to chauffeur

There is no intrinsic *up* movement which you need follow. As Dr. Harold Leavitt, a professor of industrial psychology, says: ". . . perhaps a person should reach his peak of responsibility very early in his career, and then expect to move downward or outward into simpler, more relaxing kinds of jobs." Take your pick. When the productive life of a technical person is under ten years, there isn't so much pressure on you to have the experience. If something was just invented yesterday, you know as much about it as the other guy. The climate is perfect for total career change.

THE POSITION ABOUT THE POSITION

There is no position which is intrinsically better or more fun than another. It rests on your own experience of who you are, and what works for you. There are no other standards. But be prepared, because in this world there's not much agreement on that.

All you need to realize is that the things that give *you* pleasure and satisfaction are the things you should add into your personal job recipe. That's why today's workworld is so exciting. With the immense variety of job possibilities, it allows for a lot of tastes.

REMINDERS AND REFERENCES

Reminders

- You can make a difference in the quality of your worklife.
- You are in the middle of an opportunity revolution, with millions of exciting jobs being added every year.
- It is not the most qualified persons who get the best jobs; it is those who are most skilled at job-finding.

References

28 Days to a Better Job (particularly days one to six) by Tom Jackson. Hawthorn Books, New York, 1977.

What Color Is Your Parachute by Richard Bolles. Ten Speed Press, Berkeley, California, 1977.

Making Vocational Changes: A Theory of Careers by John Holland. Prentice-Hall, New York, 1973.

Working by Studs Terkel. Avon Books, New York, 1975.

Note: By actually doing the tactics in this book as you go along, you will translate theoretical abstractions into practical reality for yourself. Are you willing to do this?

2

WHO ARE YOU, AND WHAT ARE YOU GOING TO DO ABOUT IT?

Elsa From

I wasn't always a hairdresser. I used to be a nurse. Really. My mom had been a nurse before she married dad and quit. She always wanted me to do it. She bought me nurse caps, and little hospital stuff, and I had sick-baby dolls and a stethoscope. And if I was ever sick, forget it. She would darn near put on a uniform. She would take my temperature, write it down on a card, and bring me pills in a little cup. While "General Hospital" played on the TV, it's a wonder I didn't grow up wanting to be a permanent patient!

But, like mother like daughter! I did real well on my regents exams, and I was able to go to Monroe County Community College for Nursing. It was a two-year program, and very difficult. I got out of school in '72 and got a job not far from home in Rockland County Hospital. I hated it. The hours were terrible, and the work was very hard. We were always on the move, taking this patient down to the recovery room, holding that one's hands, handling a hundred different prescriptions, making beds. There wasn't a moment to just sit down and have a chat. Of course, mom loved it—she would not let me bitch about it at all. It wasn't all bad, of course. I was helping people and using my education, which is something. But frankly, it wasn't for me.

After a couple of years at the hospital, I had it out with my mother. We had a big fight. I told her that I didn't like nursing, that I wasn't going to do it anymore, that it wasn't me. I felt terrible about quitting. It was like throwing away something you've saved up, but I knew that if I stayed there I would just get more resentful. Mother came out of it all right, finally. It was our first really big argument, and it got her to see that I wasn't her little child anymore. And I realized that, too. From then on the decisions were mine, sink or swim.

After I quit, I had the blues for a couple of months. I took some time off and went up to Woodstock with some friends, and just hung out for a while. That was nice, but I couldn't help thinking that they would all go back to work at the end, and what I would go back to was more vacation. Weird feeling.

When I got back home I sat around for a few weeks still feeling sorry for myself, wondering what kind of job I could do or wanted to do. It was hard to focus on it. Jobs all seemed alike. I didn't have a clue about them.

My friend Bob, from the Woodstock trip, invited me to New York City for a week and I went. I had to get away to clear my mind. While I was there Bob set me up with this friend of his who is a career counselor, and I had a couple great sessions with her. One of the things she had me do was go through this five-page thing she had, an exercise I guess you call it, or a process. Very interesting. I had to make lists of things about myself, what did I like to do, what didn't I like, what were my skills, my interests, where did I want to live. I got to find out a lot of things about myself. Stuff I already knew, but better organized. Fascinating. I don't understand why we never did this in school. You know most of us never really look at ourselves, we just do what someone else tells us. Someone's mother wants them to be a nurse so they are, or a kid gets an erector set and his dad praises him for something he builds, and twenty years later he's a famous bridge builder.

Anyway, this woman and I went over these lists of things about me, boiled it down, and came up with a half-dozen things to look for in a job. I don't remember the list now but working with my hands was one thing, direct contact with people was another. Something about sales. Several other things.

Anyhow, I came up with a long list of jobs that fit in with things I liked to do, boiled it down to some job targets, and started to look.

Hairstyling wasn't on the list. But there were a few things like it, and so I was primed when my friend Sue told me about this very mod hairstyling salon that she and her brother were starting. I got very interested and asked her if I could be involved. It sounded great and actually hit a lot of the things that I had found out about myself.

I had to go back to school for six months, going full-time during the day, but it was fun. Now I can't wait to go to work each morning. I really do a great job, make close to $250 per week, meet lots of people, can take off time when I need to, and more than that I feel that it's my job. I created it.

TACTIC #4

If you have worked, list your past two jobs—each on the top of a sheet of your workbook—and then under each job title, list every duty or task included in that job.

When you have listed each work duty, select the two that you enjoyed the most—and the two that you enjoyed the least. Then write a paragraph for each describing why you enjoyed it, or didn't like it.

COMPLETION CHECK ☐

THE STARTING LINE

The job search starts with a journey inward. You may have been ready for us to hand you your ticket, pat you on the back, and tell you about a good job down the road. Sorry. You aren't ready for that. You already know what you want? Good, just put it aside for a few more days, and let's check it out together.

Probably the single biggest oversight or error in the job search is in this area of self-exploration and job targeting, or career planning as it's sometimes called. People resist looking very long and hard at themselves.

They are afraid to challenge their self-image, to penetrate the protective veil of attitudes, opinions, and rules with which they have become familiar.

And yet invariably, when one pierces the resistance and takes a look, the result is personal expansion and growth, more consciousness, and the potential for more satisfaction. The payoff can be immense. An early change in direction can transform a person's experience of themselves and their work, give them new directions and new games to play.

Most people will automatically seek out a particular job title which fits their picture of themselves (their role) rather than risk another work area which could be more satisfying and enriching to them. This is one of the problems of people leaving school to enter the work-world. They have inherited and developed a catalog of roles from their family, or childhood heroes, or media images. They have a fully developed slate of who the "good guys" are. But they haven't directly experienced these roles themselves, and are often not even consciously aware of the fact that they are beginning to act them out automatically. In many cases, they have very little sense of the reality of a given role, what values it holds for them, and what its costs are. This is what accounts for a lot of the confusion and masked fear which stalks schools around graduation time.

TACTIC #5

Think of five people whose jobs you would like to have, even if you don't know them personally. List the names of these people and their jobs, and then write a paragraph for each describing what it is you like about their job.

COMPLETION CHECK ☐

What most often happens is that people succeed in establishing themselves in a role, and then, one day well into it, they wake up and ask themselves, *"What the hell am I doing here?"* What comes up then is a little voice in the back of their head which says, "Too bad, Charlie, this is it. You can't turn back now, it's too late, you've got the bills to pay, the mortgage, the kids. Charlie, stop thinking and get back to work!"

You are not now, nor will you ever be, your job title.

Underneath the roles which you play out is a very healthy, feeling, thinking, sensing being who is all right just the way she or he is, and who doesn't need a role to guide her or his behavior. This person is able to identify what she or he likes and doesn't, what skills she or he has or doesn't have, and how she or he can make a contribution.

The purpose of this chapter is to take a look at this essential self, and start to get in touch with your real capacities, abilities, and interests. The goal is work satisfaction and aliveness, not role playing.

TACTIC #6

Start a new page in your workbook, and list at least 25 things you like to do whether at work or not. List anything that occurs even if you consider it very basic such as driving or cooking or writing reports or letters. List everything.

COMPLETION CHECK ☐

PLEASURE PROFILE

Q. What's the difference between work and play?
A. Well, work is difficult and physically demanding.
Q. Just like mountain climbing?
A. Well, that's not work, that's play.
Q. Again, what's the difference between work and play?
A. Work is something that you have to do.
Q. Like sleeping and eating?

WHO ARE YOU?

A. No, but work has elements of labor, and a schedule.
Q. How about research, or programs, no heavy labor there?
A. You're right.
Q. What's the difference between work and play?
A. Work is boring.
Q. Who makes it boring?
A. It doesn't matter. It just is.
Q. Like camping out for a week?
A. No, dummy, like stacking paper clips.
Q. What's the difference between work and play?
A. Work is a *drag*, they make you wear a coat and tie, get there on time.
Q. Like a dance or a wedding?
A. This is getting nowhere.
Q. You're right.
A. Say, what *is* the difference between work and play?
Q. I don't know, I've been trying to find out. I don't think there is any.

The difference between work and play is what you call it. It is really that simple. There are a few other elements which we'll look at, but get the idea that many of the same activities will shift from work to play and back depending on your position about them. If you have to fly cross country for *work* you are likely to be preoccupied, not liking it, not having much fun. But if someone gave you your own private DC-10 and crew, and you had them fly you around, the same flight would be a real "trip."

A major element is the question of choice. If someone *makes* you do something, it's a chore. The same task created by you for your own purposes is pure play. Turning work into play is as simple as deciding what you want to do, and choosing a job which will allow you to do it.

Choice comes in two flavors: You can decide what you want to do, and then go out and find it, or you can notice what you are already doing, and choose that.

In this book we're dealing with the first category of

choice, although we support both positions, and know that each can be satisfying.

Translating your top pleasures into work can be done easily. It is done all the time by actors, food critics, porn stars, ski instructors, yacht captains, craft makers, artists, and other workers.

TACTIC #7

With what criteria would you evaluate a particular job opportunity? List five or more specific criteria (e.g., advancement, location, salary, working with people), which would be personal measures of satisfaction.

COMPLETION CHECK ☐

YOU ARE NOT YOUR JOB TITLE

You are probably starting to get the picture that a job title isn't what it seems, yet many people see the job as the title. They are bound and determined to achieve the title at all costs. A writer friend went through this recently. She knew that writing was "it." She wouldn't accept any other permanent job—good, bad, or indifferent. As a matter of fact, she would take the least attractive temporary jobs so that no one would think for a moment that she had stopped being the suffering writer. She was obviously acting out a very strong role.

After much confrontation with an expert job counselor, she began to analyze the job target and see that it was made up of its own components: working alone, using her imagination, becoming famous, meeting interesting people, having a steady royalty income, etc.

When she was finally willing to look beneath the surface, she saw that there were half a dozen other jobs which could meet most of the criteria she had set up.

By going beneath the job title to its building blocks of skills and interests we break its structure apart and open the way for creating new structures, new job targets, all of which contain the pleasure of ...

DREAM JOBS

They really exist.

- Close your eyes for a minute and get a picture of yourself in an *ideal* job. Go ahead—do it.
- Close your eyes for another minute and picture another *ideal* job for yourself.
- Now do it again, and this time see if you can pick up the following details:
  What does the workspace look like?
  How are you dressed?
  What tools or equipment are you using?
  What other people are around?
  What problems are you solving?

  Relax—close your eyes, fantasize.

A dream job is one that seems so outrageous that your first instinct is to say: "Why bother? I could never get *that* job." But, the job that fits your fantasy pictures does have a place in the real world. An important thing to understand about dream jobs is that what's ideal for one person may be a drag for someone else.

Here are some dream jobs which people in a recent workshop came up with:

- To work for a travel guide and get to go all over the world.
- To be a saucier at a four-star restaurant.
- To be an elected official.
- To be in a secluded cabin, writing and getting paid for it.
- To be a costume designer for Broadway, or the movies.
- To be a well-paid fashion photographer, or work for *Penthouse* magazine.
- To work for Ralph Nader.
- To be a traveling auditor.

TACTIC #8

> List three dream jobs—jobs which would give you maximum pleasure, but which are so far out that you instinctively feel that you would not be able to get them.
>
> COMPLETION CHECK ☐

How do we know that you will actually get your dream job? We don't. What we do know is that someone will get it, and that all you need to do is to be willing to accomplish the steps between where you are now and the ideal. All this really requires is a sense of purpose. A purpose is a *direction*, not a specific goal. *If you are organized, and have a clear sense of your work purpose, you can use everything that gets in the way, every obstacle, as a way of contributing to the achievement of your purpose.*

For example, every time you find that there is a requirement or connection, or needed skill that you don't have, this clearly helps your purpose, since now you know the next thing you need to handle. Keep on trucking, one step at a time.

Warning: Don't make the mistake of thinking that when you get the dream job you will have suddenly arrived in job heaven. No way. When most people finally "make it" their first reaction is inevitably "This is it?" and a big depression sets in. Dream jobs or ideal jobs are only valuable in the sense of direction they provide.

PROBLEM SOLVING

A job is a formal opportunity to solve problems.

It is not just a list of duties, or a title or a place to go. It is, at its most basic, a problem-solving situation. Most job titles don't tell you much about what is done, what the results are, what the purpose of the job is, or what the problems are.

WHO ARE YOU?

To fully understand the meaning of a job at any level —potential employer, manager, interviewer, worker— you need to go beyond the description to the purpose of the position. When you start to do this, you open up a greatly expanded understanding of what's involved, and how you fit into it. For example, what do the following job titles mean?

Account executive
Administrative assistant
Media planner
Project engineer
Production coordinator
First-line manager
Management trainee

What do they tell you about the daily nine-to-five routine, the communications required, the resources, the stress? Virtually nothing. Of course, if you have worked as an administrative assistant you will have an idea— that it's just like your old job—and this could be very wrong.

Frequently the job title indicates that a manager has already decided how a particular problem should be solved. By listing all the skills he is looking for, he is laying out his already decided way of solving that particular problem. Even if you don't have the particular skills called for, once you find out what the underlying problems are, you may be able to see how your own particular combination of skills could solve the problems.

We will never run out of problems in our lifetime. That's a promise. (It's a safe bet when you realize that just about every solution creates at least two more problems, but that's another story.)

Who you are in work terms is a problem solver—a person who can produce specific results, given specific situations. The problems don't have to be complex, or the solutions intricate and brainy. Problem solving skills include driving a car, hemming a dress, programming a computer, typing a letter, organizing files, speaking clearly, editing, running a tractor, raising money, and selling.

You can reduce even the most complicated high-level

jobs to very simple problem-solving skills. Keep looking into the task for the next simplest level of activity, then pull apart that activity and see what skills are called for there. For example, an advertising media planner has a number of tasks, one of which is *presenting cost per thousand (CPM) figures on advertising plans*.

Breaking this down, we see that in order to accomplish this the planner needs:

- To consult the client's overall budget sheet.
- To consult *Standard Rate and Data* or space/time sales people for media costs.
- To consult Nielsen and Arbitron reports for listener strength of various scheduled spots.
- To divide media cost by readers/listeners to determine CPM—cost per thousand.

Breaking this down even further, we see that familiarity with ratings reports could be acquired by someone with a reasonably analytical mind in about six hours of coaching. We could go even further to show the type of personality most likely to be able to perform this job accurately and professionally.

Even in fairly technical jobs, we see after task analysis that about 70% of the job is nothing more than basic skills such as:

Communicating clearly
Obtaining feedback
Applying correction
Monitoring results
Targeting
Budgeting
Managing time

Beneath their fancy titles, most jobs stem from the same problem-solving roots.

YOU—THE PROBLEM SOLVER

TACTIC #9

> Now, list 25 things which you can do, problems which you can solve, results which you can produce. Don't stop short. Keep pushing until you get 25. Don't be surprised if you get some which are also on the list you created of things you like to do. That's the way it should be.
>
> COMPLETION CHECK ☐

Objection: "I knew it would come to this. Before you even ask, I've got to tell you that I know how to do very few things. I've only finished school, and it wasn't one of the best. And even though I had decent grades, I've forgotten everything I learned."

Communication received. And it's OK. You can bail out now if you want. Pass the book along. If you're panicked because you don't feel that your skills are worth a damn, you're in good company. Roughly the same reaction was registered recently by a large group of MIT alumni, some of them out of their honored school for over 15 years and drawing down salaries in the high five figures. One of the recurrent themes was fear of having very few marketable skills.

We weren't that surprised. Particularly at the highest levels, people have resistance to listing their skills. Everyone feels it might be discovered that they aren't as qualified as people think. *When you come right down to it, most jobs, even the more demanding ones, can be expressed in rather basic skill terms.*

Stay in the game.

MORE SUCCESS

Success is a promise which is never kept. It is always *out there.* The only way that many people can deal with their own pain or disappointment at the place (or state) that they are in now is to justify it in terms of possible future success or achievement.

Bob Robinson (Law Firm Associate)

This job has been a drag for the past few years. I'm waiting until I complete my J.D. When I have that, I think I can become a partner, and then I'll get to handle the kinds of cases that are really worthwhile. I won't have to put up with all this horseshit around here.

Jeannine Carris (Law Firm Junior Partner)

I thought that when I made partner, things would automatically get better. Very naive. As a new partner, I do virtually the same things as when I was an associate. Oh, I get to go to a few meetings. I've got a better office. I make a little more money; not as much more as I thought. The people who really have it made are the guys who have been around longer. The senior partners. They get to travel all over the world, work on the really good cases, and they pull down really big dollars. You've got to stick it out. You can't quit when you are a partner. You've got too much invested.

Ken Riles (Law Firm Senior Partner)

I wonder what my partners would say if they knew I was behind in my taxes. You would think that $80,000 a year would be enough. There is never enough in this damn game. I guess I sound a little bitter. I've been at this for 18 years now, and I'm getting bored. How many SEC registrations can you do in your life without going blind? And how many business lunches can you put away? I've got to lose 20 pounds or else, the doctor says. They bring these young kids in right out of the best law schools. They work their asses off for five years or so, and become partners at some point. Those that don't are practically finished, back to the minor leagues with them. When they make partner, it's another five years or so until they get any responsibility. After 15 years they're really part of the firm, but that doesn't mean they'll like it. No guarantees.

I don't really mind the work that much. The money's good but most of us spend everything we make anyway. It's just that the repetition gets to me. I have this idea that some big company will come along and put me in as an Executive VP or President, or I'll get a post in Washington. It happens, you know. That's where the action is.

SATISFACTION

As we said: *Success is the promise which is never kept. Satisfaction happens only in present time: Now. Now. Now. Now.* Moment by moment. You can't satisfy appetites with future bread. You can't experience future joy.

Work satisfaction is having a job which works for you. Now. A job which allows you to be. *Now.* A job which supports your own inventory of interests and skills. *Now.* A job in which you can play. This doesn't mean that you can't have a future purpose (we encourage you to). It does mean you must make sure that the path you are on has room in it for your own day-by-day personal, deep-felt sense of satisfaction and aliveness.

TACTIC #10

Now go back to your "I like" list from Tactic No. 6. Select the five items on the list which you now identify as your top interests or likes. Write them in your notebook. Next, select the top five things which you can do to produce results, from the list prepared in response to Tactic #9.

COMPLETION CHECK ☐

SURVIVAL

Most of what we do in life is in response to the big, unrelenting number one fear/need: survival. Somehow we don't think we're going to make it. We can get three degrees with honors from a top ten school, and we wake up in the morning knowing it won't work out. We can get a great well-paying job, and know that it's not enough. We're still in jeopardy, so we try harder. We've been taught that the key to survival is hard work. Make yourself indispensable, build security. Pensions, retirement, social security. Money. More money.

If you're reading this book now, you have handled survival. There is little question about your being able to make it to the end of the game. All of your effort, discomfort, sacrifice, hard work, putting up with, making do, skimping, saving, cheating, hustling, hoping, plotting, and planning will probably not add one day to your life. You have survived, and like most of us, refuse to believe it.

What's the survival payoff? Just take a look around:

- A civilian Pentagon worker has put in 25 years, hates his work, but wants to play out the last 5 years to retirement. His stooped body reflects his uncommunicated anger and resentment.
- A widowed schoolteacher is in constant fear of being laid off and is afraid to take chances or to be innovative in her job. "I can't afford many mistakes," she says.
- An executive is in what he sees as "the danger zone" but he has worked so long for the same company that he doubts his own abilities in the outside world.
- A plumber works six days a week and complains about having worked all his life to build a good business. Now that he has, he doesn't know what to do with it.
- A garment center manufacturer has made a fortune. He has a house in the country, an apartment in the city, and two months a year off. He's bored to tears.

They all survived.

We have nothing against you handling your survival

WHO ARE YOU? 39

needs. We have nothing against you making lots of money. This book will help you do both.

And we want to open the space for you to *live* at the same time you survive. You can use your worklife as an opportunity to continually express yourself in the world in a way which brings you a direct day-by-day experience of satisfaction, *and* a good paycheck. At the same time, you can contribute value to others.

TACTIC #11

This is the synthesis of your top five "I likes" and "I cans" as uncovered in Tactic #10. List them in the form of a grid—with five skills down the left-hand side, and your five interests across the top. Then draw horizontal and vertical intersecting lines. This will create 25 intersections of a skill and interest. Select 10 of these intersections, and for each, invent or recall two or three possible jobs utilizing the intersecting skill and interest. The result is a list of 20 to 30 job titles created from your own skills and interests.

COMPLETION CHECK [ ]

LIFE PLANNING

As we've said before, there is no job title which describes who you are. You are not definable in such limited terms.

You are an ever-changing inventory of skills, interests, aptitudes, ideas, causes, needs, values, fantasies, lies, stubbornness, motivation, handicaps, advantages, connections, resources, good ideas, and bad ideas. You live in a world which is exploding with potential and change. Every solution carries the seeds of new problems.

You will have a direct relationship with the workworld for 70% of your organic life, and the way that you handle this worklife will have a direct payoff in the only coin worth having: satisfaction, growth, contribution, and self-discovery. The way you handle work will also determine the money you make, the people you know, and where and how you live.

It is a big game which requires some long-term strategies to score well.

Kenny Ada

I was a glorified bellhop when I went to college. Not that glorified, actually. I worked at the Bellevue Stratford in Philadelphia before they closed it. When I was in the army, I told them that I had hotel experience, and they put me in the food services area. I got to work in menu planning, budgeting, mess-hall operations, and so forth.

When I got out, it seemed easy to stay in the food service area, so without much looking around I took a job with a local fast-food chain which had stores from Atlanta through Durham. I did this for four years without a spectacular rise in fame and fortune. It was really just a replay of my army experience, except the hours were better.

Then I met this fast-talking cookie from California who was sales director for a new string of franchised party equipment rental places. It looked like a good way to fatten up the old bank account, so I took it. Fast food, fast money. What's the difference, right?

This chance of a lifetime lasted for about two years, not counting the three months which I never got paid for when the company collapsed.

My next job was taken out of panic. Assistant Manager at the Redwood Club. I felt it was my way to jump back on the bandwagon in food, but when I reported I found that the entire food and bar had been contracted out and my connection with it was mostly in terms of booking banquets and supervising our staff. The salary was embarrassing.

Now I'm doing better financially, but I've had to start over. There's nothing wrong with insurance, it's an immense field, but I feel as though I've just drifted in on the tide. No plan. I'm learning what kids right out of school are learning, and it's embarrassing. I've got to sit down with someone soon to start planning my career. Better late then never.

Cecilia Rabet

You would not believe how on your toes you have to be in this business. It's incredible. I mean publishing used to be about books and authors. Today, it's about packages. When I got into it from college, I knew that this was my field.

My first job was as an assistant copy editor for three months in the summer, or rather as an assistant copy editor/typist/messenger. I had planned to go back to school for my master's, but in August I canceled out. That was ten years ago, and I'm still going strong with this love affair with publishing.

I have done it all. Literally—no pun intended—from copy to production to sales. I spent a year out in the field calling on retail outlets.

I've had six jobs with two publishers and my new job as a literary agent is the most exciting so far. And it is according to plan. I want to keep on top of every new development, look it over carefully, and keep aligning my own personal strengths with what's happening in the industry. Every July or August I sit down, generally on my vacation, and take a look at my job. I list the stuff I like, what I don't like, what things I want to accomplish, what I want to find out more about. When things start to get stale, I put in some changes in direction. I feel that I will be an executive with a major firm within five years. Which one? Ask me this time next year, and I'll tell you.

A life plan is not a blueprint of your career carefully worked out and followed exactly. Rather, it is a battle plan, constantly revised and updated. It *is* a plan, however, and once established or revised, is to be followed. It starts with your personal objectives, (what continues to bring you satisfaction and reward), it includes an ongoing appraisal of what works and doesn't work, what new skills you would like to acquire, what your salary targets are, and when you (realistically) plan to achieve them.

If you are willing to go through the amount of effort required to put your life plan in writing, to revise it once a year *(keep all old versions)*, and stick with it between revisions, you will see your direction and intention appearing. The power to be master of the job game comes from knowing and living this direction and intention.

Warning: Do not try to overplan the future. Specific job targets for more than five years ahead are too far removed from present experience for most of us.

A five-year work goal is good, and can be reasonably specific (for example, assistant publisher for one of the top 20 firms). A ten-year goal must be more general (top executive). Your life purpose and direction can be clear regardless of where you stand presently in the career ladder. (For example, purpose: to influence the quality of people's lives through publishing books which create tangible value for the individual and society. Subpurpose: to keep my earnings at least 25% above the average for my college class.)

TACTIC #12

Look over the results of previous tactics, particularly the list of possible jobs uncovered in Tactic #11. Select one of these or another ideal job target that you would be happy to see yourself in five years from now. Write it down. Under this, list a job you would need to be in three years from now, to be on target for your five-year ideal target. Under this, list the entry point for you to start the ball rolling toward your three-year goal.

COMPLETION CHECK ☐

THE SPECIALIST

The more specialized a particular job is, the easier it is to locate it precisely, to define how you can produce value in it, and to communicate about it. It is also easier for you to become obsolete when a new process or technology, or political change, or whatever eliminates what you've been doing. Some engineers have been having this problem for a long time. They spend four years polishing an up-to-the-minute space or defense technology, work at it for three or four years, become an expert on, say, "explosive decompression escape hatch release mechanisms," and then one day discover that the space race has been canceled or de-emphasized, and along with it, the need for experts on hatch releases.

There is a dilemma here which traps many: *You need to have a specialty to get a good job, but if you're a specialist you run the risk of obsolescence.*

The way out of the dilemma is to continually upgrade your specialty. Keep your eye on what's happening in your field, where the growth and change are, what the most obvious areas for realignment and breakthrough are. Become a member of the professional society that relates most clearly to your field. Keep your reading of trade journals and relevant books up to date. Keep expanding the game. If you have selected a workfield which represents you, your energy in this field will continue to propel you forward beyond obsolescence.

IS THE NEW WORK REVOLUTION FOR YOU?

So far, this book has asked you to address a new reality. You have been asked to look at the workworld in a new way. The tactics and self-discovery exercises may have been difficult, and you may have felt reluctant to complete some of them. Revolutions aren't easy, and most of us would rather stay put than tinker around with our destiny.

The prevailing wisdom is simple: You go to school,

you find a job—if you're lucky, it's a good one—you stay in that job until things get so bad you quit in desperation, or they fire you in anger. You find another job, and repeat the cycle a few times. If you have any real bad problems, perhaps you see a counselor or a shrink to straighten them out. By trial and error you finally make a decent living, and then retire to talk about the good old days.

To embark on a self-directed search for rewarding and satisfying work is still a relatively rare occurrence. Your parents never did it, most of your classmates haven't done it, and even if a co-worker has started the process, he's not talking about it.

More and more schools are conducting classes in career and life planning. More books about the job search and the quest for fulfillment are available. The Sunday newspapers in major cities around the country have dozens of ads for high-priced guidance and counseling sessions. Mid-life change, career planning, and other career-related topics are becoming part of management training curricula.

You, too, are on the leading edge of this fundamental change in the way that people perceive themselves in the workworld. You are an innovator, a trailblazer, a revolutionary. The fact that you picked up a book to get some perspective on the job search puts you way out front—among the less than 10% of job seekers who are willing to seek outside aid.

Your willingness to look at the possibilities, do the exercises, and target what you want will carry you further still in this life probe. We know you can use some reassurance: *The self-directed work search technique works.*

After one series of workshops we conducted a few years ago, the state of California tracked the job experiences of the 500 participants. They found that of this group, most of whom had been unemployed for over six months, some 40% had located new and satisfying jobs—most within 60 days after the last workshop.

Knowing what you want and going out to get it is not that difficult. You may find that you feel reluctance, resistance, and discomfort associated with the material

WHO ARE YOU?

in this book. Often you may consider the steps to be useless or irrelevant. A job target which you have come up with will suddenly feel impossible: no one would hire you to do *that*. You will want to put down the book, and race to an employment agency instead. You will get bored. You may decide to take the next job that comes along, and reserve the approaches in this book for later in your life when you have more time.

Everybody looks for excuses. We'd all like to blame someone or something else for our worklife. Here are a few of the most frequently used excuses:

> I'm too young.
> I don't have the right experience.
> There are no jobs.
> My field is not hiring.
> I don't know what I want to do.
> I have no real skills.
> I've had too many jobs.
> They're not hiring blacks.
> They're not hiring women.
> I'm too old.
> I'm overqualified.
> The unemployment rate is 7%.
> This is a hard-hit area.

TACTIC #13

List at least five barriers or excuses which you feel could get in the way of your own job search. These can be internal barriers, or what you see as external barriers—list anything which you feel could stop you, or slow you down in your quest for an expanded, satisfying worklife.

When you complete the list, go back and, alongside each item, write down an action step you can take to move through or eliminate the barrier.

COMPLETION CHECK ☐

By the way, all of the above complaints may be true. Life is not fair. The world doesn't work the way we want it to. There are plenty of barriers around. You will find a lot of people who will agree with you about the barriers—misery loves company.

Having gotten this far in the self-directed work search, you have the opportunity to be either a trailblazer or a bystander.

We look forward to having you stay on the trail.

REMINDERS AND REFERENCES

Reminders

- The job search starts with a journey inward.
- Close your eyes and picture yourself in an ideal work situation. Are you willing to organize your approach to make this real? Answer yes or no.
- You are not now, nor will you ever be your job title.
- Success is something outside yourself; satisfaction is *always* right now.
- Real success is having a job which lets you play.

References

Career Satisfaction: How to Make a Habit of Success by Bernard Haldane. Acropolis Books, Washington, D.C.

Functional Job Analysis Scales: A Desk Aid Methods for Manpower Analysis No. 5 by Sidney A. Fine. W. E. Upjohn Institute for Employment Research, 300 South Westnedge Avenue, Kalamazoo, Michigan 49007.

Strong-Campbell Interest Inventory. Available at many counselling and testing centers.

PATH: A Career Workbook for Liberal Arts Students by Howard E. Figler. Carrollton Press, Arlington, Va., 1975.

Suggestion: Feeling stuck? If so, go back and do tactic 13 over again.

3

JOBS FOR THE '80s AND BEYOND

HISTORY

You are on an imaginary coach leaving Boston in 1776, horse-drawn and moving very slowly in a primarily agricultural, pre-industrial world. The population of the entire planet is under 750 million; their per capita income, around $200 per year. The workweek is 60 to 70 hours, and there is very little choice of what to do. The types of jobs available are only 20 to 30, and the work performed is essentially related to people and the physical environment. Its major component is physical labor.

By 1850 you have only just reached New York State by steam, heading for the Midwest. You're moving faster and there are more people around, but not many. World population is 1.2 billion. The work situation has changed markedly. Northeastern factory and mining towns now produce coal, iron, and textiles as well as aching backs and damaged lives. Workers are appendages of machines which drive them. Industrialization has taken root in the New World, sometimes with blatant disregard for human life and self-expression. The work ethic, fueled by "rugged individualism" and social Darwinism (survival of the fittest as a justification for greed and power), has placed increasing numbers of workers in demeaning, demanding, low-paying jobs. With few exceptions, the work you do is largely an accident of birth. If you were born among the lower classes, your working life is a prison sentence for a crime you didn't commit.

By 1925, your train has reached Chicago and you are passing through a massive railroad yard which is bustling with activity. Business flourishes as coal, iron, and steel mills expand and transportation systems are built. The work week is six days, wages are low, and unions, which began in response to poor working conditions and which experienced strong growth in previous years, are declining, as employers ruthlessly hold on to the tools of exploitation. Working conditions are irrelevant to industrial management, except when they affect productivity. A tidal wave of immigration, exceeding 500,000 working-class Europeans in this period, helps to keep wages low and competition for blue-collar jobs tight. Post-World War I liquidation of excess war-related production has left many thousands out of work —without unemployment insurance.

Even if you are in white-collar work you can expect to work your way up the hard way. There is little recognition of outstanding skills. You do what your boss tells you to do and get by on frugal wages. Job changing is rare, and is looked upon as a clear signal of disloyalty and distrust.

In 1955 you are in the Vista Dome car on the Santa Fe Transcontinental Express. You have been really barreling along and are about to arrive in Denver. World population has quadrupled, to 2.8 billion, in the seven generations your trip has taken. In the last 30 years you have witnessed the solid beginnings of worldwide industrialization and of mass consumption society. You have seen a revolution in work standards in the United States: an era of unparalleled social concern for workers, including unemployment insurance, social security, and increased trade unionism, all arising, as so much social legislation did, with the administration of Franklin D. Roosevelt as the 32d president of the United States. There have been years when the abundant receipts of the Treasury combined with hard-nosed budgeting actually created budget surpluses. You also have witnessed the brutal cleansing which went with the Great Depression of '29 when the stock market broke like an overinflated bubble and poverty and struggle reclaimed the working classes. You have seen prosperity lift off and bounce back once or twice like an overloaded aircraft trying to get airborne. Also, you have witnessed American business outstrip government and become the dominant institution of modern times.

As a blue-collar worker you have seen the minimum wage increase and mandatory hours decrease. You have experienced better heating, lighting, and ventilation, since World War II. As a man, you have been drafted, seen the world, and traveled ever since. The GI Bill got you into college, and started the boom in white-collar jobs. As a woman, you have dutifully limited your work aspirations to teaching, clerical work, and baby farming as the population soared.

The scars of the depression go deep in the consciousness of Americans. Despite the burgeoning of war-born technologies and the long, pent-up demand for consumer goods and services in 1955, your job opportunities are narrow in variety, although they are abundant in numbers. The overriding drive is just to "get a job." Workers at all levels are seen as economic units and materialism is the name of the game. *The Man in the Gray Flannel Suit* characterizes the irony of the new upward mobility: the more successfully you play the management game, the more alienated you become from your personal values and rewards.

Two hundred years after your trip began, you have screeched to a stop in Union Station in Los Angeles, removed your tie, let your hair down, and decided to hang out a bit before deciding where you want to work. You need a rest, for the last 20 years of your trip have been incredible. The world around you has tripped out. World population has doubled in 20 years. U.S. population is over 200 million and new workers are coming into the labor force in record numbers. Most of the new jobs are with organizations which produce services rather than goods. By 1976, close to 60 million of 88 million workers are in fields such as education, health care, entertainment, government, transportation, finance, insurance, consulting, or any one of hundreds of occupations producing "intangibles." The variety of products available has become literally mind-bending. The majority would be incomprehensible to the world of 50 years ago. A new political and social morality, the freedom to "do your own thing," has swept through the Western world. Society is on the move, competition is rampant, and capitalism is thriving. There is also a darker side: wells are running dry, mines need to be dug deeper, the lights are dimming. Resources are

JOBS FOR THE 80's AND BEYOND 51

running out. Productivity is leveling off. The industrial revolution appears to be winding down.

But jobs are plentiful. Although unemployment has settled in at around 7%, the scope and variety of opportunity has expanded. Technology is the genie in the lamp of postindustrial society, the beginnings of which you are experiencing.

Every newspaper brings stories of new products, inventions, and problems to be solved. New environmental, social, and political demands are created constantly. New sights and sounds, new approaches to old agenda are becoming necessary. More and more people are needed to get more and different jobs done.

A shift is occurring in man's relation to his machines. Automation, once feared as a great disrupter, turns out to be an ally of the worker. Many boring, slavish jobs are being replaced by machinery which expands productivity, profits, output, and the scope of most jobs. Accordingly, employment has moved toward more white-collar occupations: clerical, managerial, technical, and professional. Even at lower levels, the skills and training required increase each year. An unfortunate aspect is high unemployment of inexperienced youths, particularly those from impoverished backgrounds. In today's workworld, some expression of skill or ability is almost essential outside public service slots. Education and training pay big dividends.

From a 1978 vantage point, we see major differences in the way people relate to their jobs. Corporations no longer dominate the working class. Customers and workers are better organized against the massive powers of capital and government. People are no longer married to their jobs. Career divorce is possible—and prevalent.

A new spirit of *career entrepreneurship* is afoot. Job candidates know the ropes a little better and often are willing to hold out for higher salaries. Blacks and women have demanded and are getting a larger share of the management pie. A new career professionalism has arisen, stressing people's loyalty to their own development, and not to the organization that supports them. People realize that they can learn, grow, and actualize themselves through their work. Career consultants, guidance counselors, workshops, and books on job finding attempt to quench a new thirst for knowledge about how the job market works and how people can make it work for them.

The late '70s are clearly a turning point in the way man relates to work. You are a part of this new work revolution.

TACTIC #14

Make up a career which you think will bring you what you want. What are some of the questions you need to have answered about the job market or the job-finding process to allow you to develop a job campaign for that career? List five or six questions.

COMPLETION CHECK

ON TO THE '80s

Today's workforce is younger, better educated, more assertive, more mobile, more interested in and responsible for the world, less concerned exclusively with money, and more willing to hold out for jobs which are personally fulfilling.

The legacy of the mid-'60s and early '70s will influence the '80s. Personal freedom and expression, a more relaxed life-style, and an enlarged concern for social conditions are not only affecting people's personal and social relationships, but the nature of work itself. The master/servant relationship is evolving, however slowly, into a co-worker relationship.

Today's employers are also different. Top management is younger, more "hip," more willing to admit mistakes, to change the organization structure, to move in new directions, and to reward people for results. Management has found that many old structures can't handle the requirements of today's world.

A new style of management by "project group" or "task force" has become widespread after having been introduced successfully by aerospace firms and NASA to handle the requirements of complex tasks which were often of very short duration or speculative in nature. This intentional transience of organization has reached into the management style of many firms in all areas of business, and even into government. It has made employers more flexible and open to new problem-solving approaches. It has made it easier for job seekers to enter companies at an experienced level, without working their way up from the bottom. It is clear that this trend will continue in the next decade. Change, redesign, transfer, and reorganization will provide a new work approach based on the interplay of abilities and solutions.

The new workstyle will include shorter term employment, with positions lasting an average of three to four years. Movable pension rights, comfortable unemployment insurance benefits, and streamlined adult and vocational education opportunities will ease the transition from job to job and career to career. Temporary work will become increasingly popular and professional.

The demand for specialized skills will accelerate. Automation, information processing, and manufacturing control systems will make much of the drudge work obsolete. Problems and failures will be well advertised —and solutions sought in a more open way. Man will re-orient himself with the workworld virtually as an independent contractor, providing his solutions to the highest bidder. Workers who do not keep up their profession's standards will find themselves passed over, or living on the lower fringes of the social structure.

"Experience," the chronological measure of exposure to a particular work area, is on its way out as the primary measure of qualification for a job. That you have done task A for 12 years is no longer a measure of your ability to do task B, or even to continue to work creatively on task A, since the nature of problems shifts rapidly, and new tools are constantly available. If you haven't kept up with the latest techniques, you may find that a new graduate without experience, who is more up-to-date on current approaches, is competing for your job. In a world of newly created problems, the person with the answers is king.

In the 1980s we will come to fully recognize a knowledge revolution. A new kind of specialized knowledge, "skilledge," will be seen as the most negotiable form. Having "skilledge" means being fully versed in a particular area of application with a background of theory and principle from which to generate answers—and the pragmatic skills to put these theoretical answers to work. It will no longer be necessary to get a master's degree in social behavior to serve as a case worker in an inner-city ghetto, or to spend four years learning everything from comparative anatomy to chemistry in order to clean teeth. With the right skilledge, you can build your skills from a foundation of knowledge, and periodically update your knowledge based upon the requirements of the practical problem.

The demand for knowledge and skills is insatiable. Computers, electronics, health care, entertainment, space exploration, nuclear power generation, and many more modern growth industries require millions of new technology-oriented workers. Knowledge creates its own demand. Consider our experience with the transistor, the computer, plastics. Coming up next: microelectronics, solar heating, nuclear fusion, fiber optics, lasers. And breakthroughs in diet, human consciousness, education, transportation, materials, plus those things which will happen this time next year that we can't imagine today, will combine to produce jobs few can now imagine.

TACTIC #15

List three new growth areas, and under each major area list as many real or possible new job titles as you can. You should get at least ten under each heading.

COMPLETION CHECK

PLAYING THE GAME

Work is a game. It is *the* game of this era of mankind. The stakes are high, the traps and faults hazardous, and the strategies needed to succeed complex. But it is clear now that the earlier fears of man in dronelike servitude to the machine have proved unfounded. Technology *creates* jobs, and the game continues. Every new burst of practical creativity attracts a new population of workers.

The essence of a game is to get from where you are to a goal. The goal is a solution to a problem, the filling of a need, the answering of a question—or whatever it is for you. The only way to approach the game of work is as a vehicle for personal aliveness and joy; to use the experience in a way that fulfills you, and expresses you as you do it. You can enhance enormously the way you live your life, and the contribution you can make, by selecting games which relate to your basic satisfaction and abilities.

NEW TIME

A few years ago an imaginative and dedicated woman, Ina Tortin, recognizing her personal needs for a more flexible work schedule, invented a company called NewTime, Inc., to provide employees to organizations on less than a full nine-to-five basis. The foundation of her sound concept was that a large number of tasks could be handled in 15 to 20 hours per week, and that organizations were unnecessarily saddling themselves with full-time, full-salaried personnel out of an unconscious adherence to traditional work schedules.

The new employment service (and those which soon emulated it) attracted a cornucopia of jobs and employers needing everything from baseline clerical to top line management:

Clerk to catch up on filing two days a week
Restaurant shift manager
Editor for company in-plant publications

Researcher for PR firm
Telephone salesperson
Secretary to manager who is only in his office 3 days each week
Once-a-week bookkeeper
Interviewer for business school
Traveling recruiter for expanding electronics firm
Tutor
Personal shopper
Communications consultant
Fund raiser
Guidance counselor at a drug clinic

The people who came in for jobs included housewives whose children no longer needed them full-time, newly marrieds, and a smattering of creative types attached to low-paying writing or acting professions.

As word got around, a not so obvious group showed: people whose life-styles included professional studies, strong avocations or hobbies, or just plain laziness.

You should know that there is no need to be tied down to a full-time job—unless you want one. Permanent work on a part-time basis is something you can use to develop new skills, to fulfill your family obligations, or to limit your participation with the material realm. You can use the services of these various agencies, or find your own part-time job through the research and targeting techniques described later in this book.

TEMPORARY TIME

Another valuable way to gain experience and flexibility in your worklife is through affiliation with one of the many temporary help services. These services, which have grown from a few small local agencies in the late '40s to a thriving industry with thousands of practitioners, provide one of the best ways to develop new work skills, gain a basic familiarity with the workworld, fit into a flexible schedule, or re-enter the job market after a long absence.

Temporary help services provide help to employers

who need a replacement for a person on vacation, or workers to handle new product introduction, to fill in at workload peaks, or to supplement their regular staff for any reason.

According to Mitchel S. Fromstein, president of the largest and oldest of the temporary service firms, Manpower, Inc.: "We have some people who find this to be the only possible workstyle: housewives and mothers, students and people with seasonal professions such as teachers. Others find this to be the workstyle which gives them the kind of freedom and flexibility which they want. An assignment can last a few days to many weeks and can range from file clerk to engineer/designer." As an industry experiences changes in direction, and requires more flexibility in manpower planning, the temporary service agencies no doubt will continue to expand.

When you work through a temporary service firm, you are on their payroll and are paid weekly on the basis of the number of hours you work. There is no direct fee to you for the service: the employer pays a marked-up hourly rate.

Working for a temporary service is an ideal way for you to gain experience and improve your skills as you earn a rather basic salary. Some temporary services, such as Manpower, offer free testing and skills improvement classes, and the possibility of traveling to a new city. You can be reasonably sure of a way to quickly plug in your skills. The search for your work identity may be illuminated by temporary or part-time assignments.

BACK TO SCHOOL

There are now, and there will continue to be a substantially larger number of college-trained individuals than there are jobs requiring a college education. Ph.D. history majors with $30,000 educations will work as hotel clerks and taxi drivers until they can identify a practical work area to pursue. At the lower end of the educational strata, workers are getting squeezed out. Poor and black, entry level work candidates who are on the streets after completing high school (or dropping out) now represent 25% of the unemployed in this country.

This fits into the prevailing economic myth about employment—that there are only a limited number of jobs which are created "up there" by industry and government, so some must do without. *Don't fall for it.* Don't write off the unskilled. The route to full employment is simple—it isn't a matter of creating more slots into which more people can be plugged. In the emerging workworld, the unemployed must be trained in *two* life systems: the self-directed, introspective process of personal ability identification, job targeting in problem areas, and communication of potential value and benefit; and the skilledge (skills backed by knowledge) related to a job target area with relevant applications.

The tools to accomplish this are available. All that is needed is for the realization of the correct context of work to take root:

A job is an *opportunity* to solve a problem.

There are an *unlimited* number of problems in the world today, therefore:

There are an unlimited number of jobs to be performed.

So look at learning. Look at education as a tool to get what you want, not as something you've got to get through.

> Q. Hold it. I will not go back to school. I've had it with that crap.
>
> A. Oh, you again. You've had it with school, you say.
>
> Q. Yes. Really. Twelve years of elementary and high school, two years at the community college. God knows how many boring, tedious hours sitting on my butt listening to someone talk at me about stuff which I can't even remember now. You can keep it. Look, why not just show me how to get on with the job search.
>
> A. Yes, I know. It's not unusual to look at the school experience as one in which we are dominated, restricted, held in place, subjected to the beliefs

JOBS FOR THE 80's AND BEYOND

and opinions of our teachers. In school we are rarely praised or acknowledged; almost never given a full sense that we are OK. We are starved for a purpose or direction of our own. The experience is not always an enlightening one.

Q. Thank you. That's how I feel about it too.

A. And yet your experience of school is not necessarily your experience of learning.

Q. What do you mean?

A. Do you have any hobbies or play any sports?

Q. I'm not much for sports, but I do play tennis. My only real hobby, I guess, is cooking. I love to cook and eat really fine food.

A. Great, sounds like a possible job target there. Did you ever take any cooking lessons?

Q. As a matter of fact, I have. I studied Chinese cooking for two evening semesters with Virginia Lee.

A. Did you like it?

Q. How could I not like it? New dishes to learn, new tastes to explore, it was fun. I never got bored. I couldn't wait to try new recipes on my friends.

A. How would you explain the difference between your cooking lessons and say, learning algebra?

Q. Easy—algebra doesn't taste good! Seriously, there was nothing about algebra that had any reality for me. I didn't know where or when I would even use it, why I needed to know it.

A. What else?

Q. I don't know. I didn't like the regimentation, the fact that you had no choice in it. If you could give kids a choice about algebra very few would pick it on their own, I bet.

A. Do you think that education would be a different experience if you were able to have more choice in it?

Q. It would be totally different, but I don't think it would work. Kids don't know what they want.

A. But as an adult?

Q. As an adult you have a better idea, but still, most people don't know what they want.

A. But if you ever did get clear about who you were, and what you wanted to do, where you

wanted to go, do you see how interesting and
valuable the right course could be?

Q. Yes. If I wanted to take a six-month sailing trip,
I would go out of my way to find a good course
in navigation, and I wouldn't miss a class. I
would stay with it as though my life depended
on it.

A. Yes, because it would.

Q. Or I could go for something I really was
interested in, like tennis, or Chinese cooking.

A. Yes, like Chinese cooking.

Education seen as a tool to get what *you* want is an entirely different experience from education as a device to give you what *they* want.

In the coming years of your worklife, as our society becomes more and more involved in cleaning up the messes we make, handling our environment, husbanding our resources, and moving in the direction of experiencing our own aliveness and well-being, it will become more important for you to keep yourself on top of the technologies associated with the work areas you have selected. You can look on this as ongoing training and education to support your present work, or as a springboard to the next position with more salary and more responsibility—or to a totally new career.

This object-directed continuing education can be obtained in many ways, through formal programs in the existing educational structures, or informally, through your relationships with experts in your field. Develop an instinct to head *toward* problems rather than away from them.

ACCORDING TO SOURCES

Throughout the rest of this chapter we will be describing work areas that are expected to expand over the next five to ten years, according to official government sources. We will also give some observations—by us and others—which are anything but official.

The official information has been derived from the U.S. Department of Labor's Bureau of Labor Statistics, and particularly from their premier publication on jobs, *The Occupational Outlook Handbook*. This telephone directory-size publication describes 850 occupations and 35 industries, giving facts about job titles, duties, employment level predictions, educational and training requirements, and earnings. It also indicates valuable sources of additional information and training in the fields described. Copies are available in most libraries and career information centers, or from the government.

Professionals have faced a problem for years with *The Occupational Outlook Handbook:* how to use it to assist people in determining their career, or for that matter, how to use the speculative and statistical information prepared by legions of agencies, universities, or consultants (usually with almost no input from the employers themselves!). To pick a job target because of a future projection is about as safe as buying commodity futures. Even if there will be a strong demand in a field you don't like, that is no reason to make it your goal. Nor should you necessarily be deterred from a field because there appears to be a shortage of openings. Most of our top performers (theatrical and others) would never have been heard of if they followed the conventional wisdom of supply and demand.

There would be at least an advisory value to the predictions in relationship to the individual if these volumes were more reflective of the dynamic and rapidly evolving work opportunities that exist in society.

However, after you have uncovered specific job targets related to your own skills and interests, and have located them in the contemporary world, it does make sense to see what the Bureau of Labor Statistics says about your selection. Note that it tends to overgeneralize in many categories, so you may have to stretch to find your own particular area.

There are many trends in employment which are valuable to watch. Total employment is predicted to reach 110,688,000 jobs in 1985. This growth is primarily a function of technology and, secondarily, a reflection of more women entering the workforce, and undoubtedly (not apparently foreseen by BLS at this time) will be further expanded as compulsory retirement regulations are rescinded and people over 65 get to stay in the game a few years more.

THE TRENDS

WHITE COLLAR

A white-collar job is one that doesn't show the dirt, and there are more of them than ever—rising to over 50% of the workforce by 1985. There are a lot of crummy white-collar jobs, so don't think that this is automatically an improvement.

CLERICAL

If you are a great secretary and love it, you won't have a job-finding problem for at least ten years—or until they perfect the word-processing voice-translating computer system, complete with coffee maker. Even then, they will probably miss the sex angle which is chauvinistically ingrained in clerical roles. It's a good place to start but a dangerous place to stay too long.

PROFESSIONAL AND TECHNICAL

This overbroad category has trends within trends: fewer teachers, more accountants, etc. Overall, if you wear a suit to work, are a college graduate, and work in a reasonably technical, nonadministrative role (engineer, therapist, doctor, lawyer, systems designer, personnel manager, etc.), you will be in a seller's market. Since "professional" hardly means anything in itself, you'd better research further before you celebrate unmitigated security. As a matter of fact, there is a whole crowd of community college and vocational school types after your executive swivel chair. Paraprofessionalism, i.e., learning just what's needed to get the job done solidly and well, is a trend that figures clearly in our vision of the future.

MANAGERS AND ADMINISTRATORS

If you can get people to align behind you, support you fully, communicate what works and what doesn't work to you and each other, and do whatever is necessary to get the job done, you are a master of management, and will be able to create jobs, demonstrate results, and work equally well in dozens of fields.

People skills are in very short supply. Training in management, communication, supervision, decision making, and corporate politics is hard to come by, and by God we need it. Do whatever you can to get trained in the marvelous areas of interpersonal communications and systems for managing change, goal setting, feedback, motivation, or correction routines. Go beyond the normal M.B.A. course work. Do *est* and TM, study TA and yoga. Read the biographies of the titans in your profession. Learn to bank on your own experience with people. Learn how to lead groups. Expand your ability to articulate clearly. With firm control of people management techniques and skills, you can expand the game in virtually any area you wish to play. Job openings for proven managers are predicted to continue to expand dramatically. But if you are just pretending, watch out for the trapdoor.

SALES WORK

A grounding in sales is one of the most important assets you can have in almost any career you choose. Long stigmatized as aggressive or "pushy," the art of selling requires strong, effective communication and knowledge of human motivation. Your abilities in this area will continue to pay dividends as the workforce expands and becomes more complex. With new directions, new problems, and new solutions, people who can present ideas to others in a way which communicates will have many opportunities.

Your ability to deal with your own career life development and job finding is also enhanced by a training in sales motivation and communication.

Participation in a sales training program provided by a blue-chip company (IBM and Xerox are excellent) is a strong credential for high-level sales work.

Retail sales and distribution jobs may not increase as dramatically, as new merchandising techniques are employed.

FARMING

Agribusiness is here. Farms are larger, machines are larger, crops are larger, food is more a product than a commodity, and the number of farmers is diminishing. To be more accurate, the number of jobs on farms has plummeted, according to statistics: mechanization has taken its toll of jobs. If you have an interest in handling hunger in the world, are able to speak a couple of languages, and know how to deliver results, there is much you can do. Nutrition is in.

SMALL BUSINESS

Fewer mom-and-pop corner grocery stores, and more consulting firms is the trend. Overall growth in the number of small, privately held firms will continue to expand, but only in areas where individual talents are important. Once an area has been formulated or mechanized, watch the big boys jump in. Franchises will continue to offer opportunity for entrepreneurs with some money.

BLUE COLLAR

Working with dirt is not popular. The media doesn't like it much. Mothers and fathers usually don't want their kids to follow them in factory or construction work. Laborers don't seem to have much fun; and, according to the statistics, we are eliminating a large number of our most physically demanding jobs. American industry, following Sweden's lead, is enriching the composition of most manufacturing, assembly, and detailing jobs which require primarily mechanical abilities.

A laborer's work, if you get beyond the bad reputation, can be a wholly satisfying way to be who you are, to work in your environment in a way which creates satisfaction for you and results for others. You may be reminded of the famous Tom Sawyer fence whitewashing incident, by the hundreds of Americans who actually pay good money to work with their hands in the blazing sun, for example, at university-sponsored archaeological digs or at Palo Solari's Acrosanti building project in Arizona. The controlling factor is *choice*. If you choose to work with your hands as a laborer, and keep rechoosing it, you are no different from a sculptor working with common materials. Laboring, factory working, and other blue-collar jobs are not inherently bad or good. Watch for even the most fundamental jobs to increase in complexity and variety. Skills pay. (See "Construction Trades" below.)

SERVICE WORKERS

With rather unfathomable logic, the Bureau of Labor Statistics includes FBI agent, police chief, beauty operator, and janitor in this category, so it is hard to give this group an overall growth rating. Police protection will unfortunately be an expanding requirement for at least the short term, until social scientists, politicians, and educators provide breakthroughs in the prevention of crime and mischief. Keep your eye on trends and public temperament and you will develop a more accurate feel for the growth of jobs in this area. In our view, anyone who can perform personal services in a way which gives the recipient a clear sense of having been served well and contributed to will continue to be very much in demand.

CONSTRUCTION TRADES

Construction activities are watched almost as closely as the stock-market averages as indicators of economic growth or decline. They are therefore almost impossible to predict over more than a two-year period, as so much depends on the national economy. Careers in this highly skilled segment of the blue-collar field require a dogged persistence which is unnerving at best. Many young workers left the field when it went from boom to bust in the early '70s. Statisticians tell us that greatly increased construction is inevitable because of population growth, while bankers tell us that demand is limited by outrageously high costs. Again, skills draw the highest cards: heavy equipment operators, metalworkers, roofers, and electricians will be most in demand.

A major problem for workers in these trades, or in other blue-collar occupations, has been their lack of knowledge and skill about how to reshape their careers, or how to refocus their skills and abilities to other areas when the building cycle is down. This "let's stick it out together" attitude has left many able, intelligent and skilled workers unemployed on the back porch for a year or more, apparently dependent on larger forces to get things moving again. With broadened exposure to workworld needs and a strengthening of their own abilities to deliver value in a shifting economy, people in these fields can experience strong, continuing opportunity.

MAINTENANCE AND REPAIR

Things don't work: the lawnmower, the TV, the tractor, the family car, the million-dollar computer system, the toaster. It's natural that as resources become scarce people will want to hold on to things longer—so they will need to have them repaired. Repairmen in fields in which they have a soundly based interest and skilledge can look for expanding opportunities with good flexibility and good money. It is especially important here to keep up-to-date with new designs and technologies. There are fine opportunities to own small profitable businesses in maintenance and repair, by the way.

THE TOP 25

Listed below are the job titles which the Bureau of Labor Statistics feels will be among the fastest growing (in terms of percentage of current employment in that field) between now and 1985 (edited by us).

Inspectors (manufacturing): more regulation, more inspection.

Water treatment operators: more push to clean up waste water.

Opthalmic lab technicians: increasing demand for glasses; includes optometrists, designers of frames.

Credit and collection workers: catching up with the cashless society.

Secretaries, typists, receptionists: keeping up with burgeoning paperwork.

Programmers and systems analysts: computers continue to expand, microcomputers are catching on.

Bank clerks and tellers: banks will provide more services, need more people to handle them.

Accountants: helping business keep up with complexities, new and financial control regulations.

Personnel and employment: new employee relations programs, human resources concerns, EEO adding to the importance of personnel.

JOBS FOR THE 80's AND BEYOND

Insulation workers: big demand to insulate in face of fuel shortages.

Carpenters: replacement and remodeling will be popular as housing costs continue to soar.

Heavy equipment operators: more mechanization of construction industry.

Plumbers: construction and growing trend toward air conditioning and other environmental systems.

Airline support personnel: lower costs, more flights are projected as people explore the world.

Engineering: all areas slated to expand; select specific fields intelligently.

Environmental sciences: a big job ahead, getting things cleaned up.

Technicians and drafters: a new awakening for technical support personnel. Must keep skills updated.

Mechanics and repairers: generally across the board, automotive, equipment, electronics, etc.

Paramedical: exploding need for assistants in virtually every medical and health field including nursing.

Medical administrators: to handle the paperwork and organization of expanding health care facilities.

Career planning and placement: will expand as schools continue to awake to the value contributed by these professionals.

Social services: hard to believe that this can continue to expand, but that's what the figures say.

Architects and urban planners: we will be cleaning up our urban centers, and functionally redesigning them.

Police officers: state and local, particularly big cities.

Libraries: public, college, university, so says BLS.

For more details in these and hundreds of other fields, consult *The Occupational Outlook Handbook*.

FURTHER OUT

As we stated earlier, and as Alvin Toffler, Peter Drucker, John Gardner, and others have pointed out indirectly, there is another, entirely different way to look at jobs: to see them in terms of the problems which need to be solved or, to look at it another way, as identified solutions seeking problems to neutralize.

For example, look at a deep massage system developed by a woman, now in her 80s, named Ida Rolf. Rolfing, as this procedure of rather painful muscle manipulation and alignment is known, has demonstrated in thousands of people results of better balance, more vitality, a more youthful body, and more physical range and dexterity.

An argument can be made that virtually anyone who is concerned about his own body (which has to be most of us) would want to go through this, since the results are so positive and so basic. Yet there are only 150 Rolfers, most with reasonably busy practices and good incomes. How many openings are there for Rolfers?

On the one hand the number is immense, since once a person is clear about the value of Rolfing, he will probably want to have it done. Therefore, each new Rolfer can within six months or a year build up enough clients and referrals to create a new job. On the other hand, there are no *announced*, advertised openings for Rolfers.

When you look at the job world from the context of problems and solutions, exciting new channels of potential open up and worklife no longer looks so stuffy. Here are some examples of day-to-day problems, large and small, that need solutions:

How to get people around conveniently with less energy and lower cost

How to create a delicious soft drink which is highly nutritious

How to get people to release the pent-up tension in their lives, relax, have more fun

How to monitor heart attacks

How to organize an office so that everyone works together, gets the job done, and likes it

How to write commercials that really communicate

How to make it easier for mothers of young children to have careers

How to produce razor blades that need to be replaced only once a year

How to bring down the cost of housing

JOBS FOR THE 80's AND BEYOND

How to truly entertain others

How to teach people so that they experience the value of learning

How to reduce traffic deaths

Here are some of the many "solutions" around looking for a problem:

People who see and hear what is really there

People who can create dreams on paper and sing them

People who will move anything anywhere

People who know what their neighbors want and need

People who could even organize a hurricane

People who understand how subways could run on time

People who can really cook

People who don't give up

People who can organize communities

People who are conscious and aware

People with the strength of a jackhammer

People who can turn a barn into a palace

People who understand astronomy

People who operate effectively even if everyone disagrees with them

People who know how bodies work

People who can talk to machines

People who can expand the lives of others

There are levels of jobs approaching in the next decade that the Bureau of Labor Statistics never heard of. They will be created by people with the ability to produce direct value with their skills, and they will be created by economic, social, and environmental problems which demand solutions.

This book shows you how to put together what you've got and what you like in a way which produces value for others, and satisfaction and aliveness for yourself.

REMINDERS AND REFERENCES

Reminders
- Take a look at the world you're in. See what problems interest you. Ask yourself which of those problems you can solve. Then choose that direction for your worklife.
- Work is solving problems and getting paid for it.
- Since there are an unlimited number of problems, there are an unlimited number of job opportunities.
- To get in touch with current problems which can be translated into jobs, visit your local library and read back issues of *Business Week, Forbes* and *The Wall Street Journal.*

References

The College Graduate Guide to Job-Finding by Arthur R. Pell. Simon & Schuster, New York.

Occupational Outlook Handbook. Superintendant of Documents, U.S. Government Printing Office, Washington, D.C. 20402, Cost: $8.00.

Dictionary of Occupational Titles. Superintendant of Documents, U.S. Government Printing Office, Washington, D.C. 20402, Cost: $12.00.

People's Yellow Pages. Alternative Careers, Box 31291, San Francisco, Ca.

Future Shock by Alvin Toffler. Bantam Books, New York, 1971.

The Next 200 Years: A Scenario for America and the World by Herman Kahn. William Morrow & Co., Inc., New York, 1976.

The Hidden Job Market—A System to Beat the System by Tom Jackson and Davidyne Mayleas. New York: New York Times Books.

Question: Are you willing to be a career entrepreneur ... that is, to get what *you* want?

4

TARGETING

YOU ARE NOT YOUR JOB TITLE (AGAIN)

Some pages back we made a big fuss to get you to realize that you are not your job title . . . that job classifications do not describe humans any more than song titles describe the music you will hear, or a city's name describes its climate.

You are a multifaceted creature who can put together a rock garden one day, and a financial report the next. You have the ability to learn new languages, wield new tools, listen to computers, and talk to God.

You are essentially restless and craving, conquering the seven seas and coveting the planets. You are a nomad, forsaking green New England hills for midwestern plains, giving up rugged seascapes, for downhill skiing, plain home cooking for topless bars, and deserting old and tired cities for the new and untried boomtowns. You have learned a hundred schemes and routines, and can pick up more. You are ready, willing, and able, though it doesn't always look that way. As a matter of fact, on any given day—to a person who hasn't seen you perform—you may easily look stuck in a rut. And sometimes you are.

The purpose of this section is to give you an insight into some of the ways that you can marshal your potential so you can put your real potential to work in the world. This procedure is called targeting or, more specifically, job targeting.

Job targeting is a process in which you look at all of your personal purposes, goals, and capabilities, and then uncover the specific work areas (out of thousands) which will best satisfy them.

It is the next step in the process we have already begun. Once you have established particular job targets which reflect who you are and what you seek, the rest of this book will instruct you in methods for obtaining these jobs.

TARGETING   73

You now have some insights about the relationship of your work to your life, and how to align the two. Using just your own knowledge of the workworld you have invented over a dozen possible positions. In this part you will add a new dimension—the outside world. You can now play the game for real stakes. Ante up.

INTENTION

A funding grant is canceled. Young Jim is let go with dozens of others. He gets a super résumé together, prints 100 copies, and buys the *Los Angeles Times* and *Wall Street Journal*. On Sunday afternoon he selects the choice advertised jobs, mails out a dozen or so résumés, then takes his wife and kids to Disneyland.

Ten days go by, and Jim hasn't heard anything. He blames the postal service and mails out half a dozen more of his slick résumés to newly advertised jobs. Then three responses arrive in one morning's mail. Jim is shattered by the cold formality of the three turndowns: "Your résumé is being retained and we will let you know if anything..."

The next day two more rejections, both on printed forms. By the end of the week he has accounted for all but four of his inquiries. All negative. In following weeks and months, Jim mails out hundreds of résumés, now twice revised. No more Disneyland.

Over six months Jim keeps score patiently: 325 résumés mailed out, 230 turndowns, 8 interview requests, of which he only took 5. No offers, no job, no ideas. Betrayed by the very system which enticed him to get into teaching in the first place, he is now driving a cab, and trying to piece together a nervous marriage. Story ends.

Jim played out his role nicely in an old familiar scenario:

> "There are no jobs out there—I've answered hundreds of ads."
> Jim, what are you looking for?
> "At this point I'll take just about anything. I've tried everything in my field."

Oh. What have you tried?

"I've mailed out hundreds of résumés for teaching jobs. If there's anything out there that I missed, I'll eat my hat."

Did you have any particular kind of thing in mind?

"What do you mean *particular*? A man can't be particular in today's job market. I answered every ad I could find."

Did you do anything besides answer ads?

"Like what? I tried a half-dozen employment agencies, but they were worthless."

Did you try anything outside of teaching—other types of jobs?

"Well, I'm sure that would have been a waste of time. If they aren't interested in my teaching skills I doubt that I could interest them in anything else, except driving this cab. It's a very tight job market around here. . . ."

"They" strike again. *They* aren't interested, *they* don't have any openings, *they* are unfair to innocent teachers. The familiar litany of the not responsible job seeker. If instead of mailing out hundreds of résumés to try to get advertised positions he had developed specific job targets, and then located the firms who could hire him in these areas, Jim would have had a satitsfying job in six to eight weeks.

THE TIP OF THE ICEBERG

A job rarely gets advertised until a firm has been unable to locate the person they seek through internal channels, referrals, friends, contacts, back files, job posting, and anything else the employer could think of to avoid the high cost of hiring by advertising.

Fully 85% of the jobs available on any given day do not get advertised. These jobs comprise the hidden job market, and this is an essential place to scout out the custom-tailored positions that we are talking about in this segment of the book.

Jim's big mistake was that he didn't have specific job

targets to go after. He, like thousands of others inexperienced in the dynamics of the job market, made the mistake of thinking that the more general his job target—in his case, *all* the advertised jobs for teachers—the more possibilities he would open up. The opposite is true.

By clearly specifying a job target in as many aspects as possible, you expand, rather than diminish, your ability to locate prospective employers.

Being without specific job targets keeps you floundering in the job stew, chasing after every carrot or potato that bobs to the surface. You lose the sense of purpose which is necessary for sustained energy.

EXPANSION

Before you can focus on specific job targets, you must expand your thinking about jobs and become more aware of opportunities in the workworld. There are a number of approaches which will assist you in this, and one of the simplest is the job family process described on the next page:

TACTIC #16

A job family is a common interest grouping of jobs described by one term. Each job family category includes dozens to hundreds of specific work descriptions, job titles, and opportunities for problem solving. For example, the automotive job family would include jobs in designing cars, selling cars, repairing, transporting, writing safety brochures, and making safety inspections, to name a few.

Shown below are 87 job families. Go through the list three times. First, draw a line through each job family which holds no interest for you. Then go back and circle each family which holds some interest for you. Then select the top four families—the ones most interesting and relevant to you.

Accounting	Family services	Paper
Advertising	Fashion	Performing arts
Aeronautics	Finance	Personal services
Agriculture	Fine arts	Personnel
Animals	Fishing	Photography
Architecture	Gardening	Physical conditioning
Automotive	Government services	Physics
Banking	Health	Politics
Bicycles	History	Public speaking
Biology	Industrial design	Publishing
Boating	Insurance	Real estate
Bookkeeping	Interior design	Recreation
Botany	Investments	Religion

Building services
Camping
Children's services
Commercial art
Communications
Computers
Construction
Cosmetics
Counseling
Crime detection
Ecology
Economics
Education
Electronics
Engines
Entertainment

Journalism
Law
Machinery
Magic
Management services
Marketing
Mathematics
Medicine
Mental health
Metalwork
Movies
Museum work
Music
Nutrition
Oceanography
Office services

Repair services
Retailing
Secretarial services
Selling
Sociology
Sports
Stamp collecting
Synthetics
Television
Textiles
Toys
Transportation
Travel
Weather
Woodworking
Zoology

COMPLETION CHECK ☐

77

TACTIC #17

List each of the four job families you selected (in Tactic #16) on a separate sheet of paper in your notebook. Under each job family list as many specific job titles, positions, opportunities, or descriptions of possible jobs as you can think of, regardless of whether they are things you feel you would like to do. List menial as well as senior jobs. Keep at it until you have been able to list at least 20 different possibilities under each.

The object at this stage is for you to continue to expand the number of possible job situations that you are aware of in a given field. If you have difficulty in coming up with a full list, get in touch with someone in the field, or read a few trade journals or books about the subject, or, call the professional association connected with the area.

COMPLETION CHECK ☐

TACTIC #18

You now have a list of 20 job possibilities in each of the job family areas which you selected. Go over each list, and cross out all those which you know you would not find personally satisfying.

Then go back over and cross out each one you feel would be highly impractical for you to identify or obtain. (Be careful here. Don't cross anything out unless you are certain that there is a very real prerequisite which you don't have.)

Then list all of the remaining tasks combined from all lists, in order of maximum satisfaction. Go down the list, one by one, and ask yourself the following question: "Am I willing to do what's necessary to get this job?" If the answer is yes, allow it to remain. If not, cross it out.

COMPLETION CHECK ☐

THE NEW OLD-BOY NETWORK
Steve Lynn

At the workshop I came up with this job target of being an advance planner. Only then I didn't even know what the job was called. I knew that big companies must have smart front-line people to help them decide where to go when they are relocating a division or plant. Advance work which would get me involved in all aspects of a community, and many aspects of the corporate/political field.

I decided to follow the personal referral network technique that we had discussed. Interviewing for information rather than directly for a job.

I first called City Hall, and found out about the Economic Development Agency, the group which keeps track of corporations that are relocating out of town. They gave me the names of VPs of three large corporations which were planning moves within the year.

I called each of them, reaching a man at a large oil company who agreed to meet with me for 15 minutes to answer any questions. I told him I was doing some research for an article, and that I was also personally interested. I really did intend to do the article, and possibly I still will. Anyway, the oil company guy was great and gave me lots of information, such as how to get into the field without the normal real estate background.

He also gave me, at my request, the names of three other people, two at other Chicago corporations and one with a well-known consulting firm.

I started to fill a three-ring binder with notes and questions to ask, and I also did some library research. Read one very good article. In *Fortune*, I think it was.

All in all I had around fifteen information-type interviews. Each one would give me expertise which I would use the next time. After eight I was an expert.

I had saved two consulting firm referrals for last. I blew one of them: the guy was either threatened by what I knew, or else he felt I was a professional spy. The other was just what I wanted. The junior partner returned my call, which was disappointing since I had wanted to meet the big guy. After our lunch, I did nothing and, sure enough, a week later I got a call at home from the senior partner.

He was warm and friendly. So was I. We met for drinks at the Princeton Club.

At the end of about an hour together he asked me if I was looking for a job. I told him that I had thought about it a couple of times, and wasn't sure I was ready yet. But what did he have in mind?

He said $14,500, and I said "Hmm." Nothing else.

To make a long story short, he finally offered $17,000, and threw in the tuition for my M.B.A. at night at the University of Chicago.

It was great fun. I got the job I wanted, learned about a new field, and made a lot of good contacts to boot. And I never even had a résumé.

You can do a faster, abbreviated version of the above personal referral network by phone, if you are able to make cold calls to a dozen people or less. Start with the Yellow Pages in virtually any subject and call the firms whose names are listed. Ask for the names of leaders in the field, trade publications, and business associations.

The new old-boy network works. You can build one in any field that you like. Just keep letting people know, directly and simply, that you are looking for advice from an expert, or information for an article or research.

TACTIC #19

Pick one of your job family areas and identify five people: authors of articles, people working in the field, and referrals. Write down some of the questions you would like to ask them—and phone each of them to find out more about what is going on in the field. Then go out and conduct this research, taking notes, and obtaining the names of others in the field.

Once you have accomplished this, you may want to consider doing it in your other job families.

COMPLETION CHECK

TARGETING

OBSTACLES

You will continually run into obstacles in your work search. Obstacles are as much a part of this game as cold weather is of football. Expect them, and don't be surprised or put off course when you find that two out of three of the people you call aren't in, or don't want to talk to you. So what? If you are committed to obtaining the results, then the disappointments and snags which get in the way will become just one more sign that you are moving along the path to your objective. If it takes three attempts to reach one person, then the calculations are simple: Be prepared to try thirty calls to reach ten.

Many people have such a deep-rooted conviction that they aren't going to make it in life that they will eagerly grasp any disappointment or obstacle as a way to prove it. In the work search this self-invalidation is particularly intense. We have been conditioned to invest so much of our self-image in our jobs that the slightest hint of a problem or possible failure will bring up our worst fears of failure.

Therapists and counselors report that job failure is one of the most common recurring fears of their clients. It doesn't matter if you are entering the job market for the first time, hoping for that promotion, or coming back to work after seven years devoted to the saintly art of motherhood. You are probably scared silly that at long last you will be found out, discovered to be the base incompetent that you have always known you are.

Obstacles, barriers, turndowns, missed opportunities, rejections, disappointment, self-reproach, unfulfilled expectations, unresponsiveness, disinterest, boredom, regret, stupidity, and fear will all occur in your job search. They are an integral part of virtually every job campaign which ever produced any positive results. Of course, you ought to know that the same human failure responses are also part of every other worthwhile, expanding activity. People who resist failure rarely succeed. People whose main purpose in life is to be comfortable rarely expand.

When you know in advance that the roller coaster ride is going to be a bit scary, there is really only one approach to take: Sit back, hold on, and enjoy it.

TACTIC #20

You will find it helpful to know in advance what personal barriers or obstacles will get in the way of your job search. List all the things which you suspect at this time might inhibit you or slow you down in your job search. List everything.

COMPLETION CHECK ☐

THE VIEW FROM INSIDE

The job search begins with a look inside. Who are you? What are your skills, interests, aptitudes, and motivations? What are your dreams? What is your reality?

The next step is to look from this internal vantage point out to the world, and identify the work areas which would allow you to express all of these components of yourself.

There is no one ultimate perfect job for you. There is only continued expansion and growth, and maintaining the inner direction and control which allow you to connect to work which you love. *Real success is having a job which works for you.*

GEOGRAPHIC IMPERATIVE

Where would you like to live? If you could have the job you want anywhere in the country, or in the world, where would it be?

Are you stuck in your own hometown because that's the place you are most familiar or comfortable with? Take a look outside. Fully 20% of the U.S. population changes location every year. We are in an enormous

TARGETING

traffic pattern, flowing from city to suburbs, from Northeast to Southwest. The U.S. labor market is truly a national market. Jobs are virtually interchangeable from community to community.

You can probably take your pick of the area where you want to live and work, and, using the techniques in this book, identify job targets there.

TACTIC #21

List 10 cities, towns or areas you have visited that you wouldn't mind living and working in. Next list 5 locations you haven't been to but would like to try.

From these 15 listings, select 4. Get a map, and locate the 4 you have selected, spot each of them, and then draw or imagine a circle 25 miles in radius. Look in the areas bounded by these circles, and see if you can come up with at least ten locations in which to focus your job search.

COMPLETION CHECK ☐

JET SET

It is definitely possible to relocate to an exciting and well-paying job outside the United States. Possible, but not easy.

The first thing you need to handle is language. The odds are 25 to 1 against you locating the kind of job target you want if you don't speak the local language well (unless you have very highly specialized skills which are in demand in the country of your choice). So, if you have aspirations without linguistics you are in for an uphill fight.

The second thing you need to deal with is the fact that most foreign nations have policies or local protectionist laws which discourage hiring foreigners except in areas where labor is in short supply. These short-supply areas tend to be grouped at the very low end of the scale (migrant farm workers, physical laborers) or in the rarefied upper atmospheres (nuclear physicist, open-heart surgeon, counterspy) and sometimes in the high-demand bilingual secretary field where looks, skills, and savoir faire can almost always open a spot legally or illegally.

Let's talk about the possibilities and approaches which will produce results despite the obstacles. It is a fact, within the free enterprise world, that *if you can demonstrate an ability to accomplish a result better than anyone around, you will probably be able to create job opportunities.* For example, if you are a specialist in 16-track recording techniques, speak enough Spanish to get by, and find yourself in Madrid one Monday morning, look up the local recording studios, call the manager and ask if you can stop by to see how *they* do it. When you see the equipment, make friends with the personnel, and feel on safe ground ask if you could stop by and assist them at a session—free of charge, of course—and perhaps show them some little things which you've happened to pick up, etc., etc. After they have a clear picture of what you can do, and how nice you are even if you *are* a Yank, let a few days float by, and then get back in touch with the manager, and let him know that you'd be willing to help him out on a more regular basis, for a modest salary.

The idea is not to bust in like gangbusters and put everyone on the defensive. Start with a clear target, something you can do to create value, locate the people who could utilize the value, *demonstrate* the value, and only then ask to be paid for it.

Look for introductions and referrals. Who do you know who knows someone who has a contact in your target country or city? Have him write or call in advance.

Look for areas where your specialized American knowledge could be of particular value to an overseas employer. It might be someone marketing goods to the United States or Canada, or someone introducing a product or service internationally which has been around for a while in your country.

Another slant, although probably not as productive,

is to locate American-based firms with offices overseas, or multinational corporations or agencies. Take inventory of your friends and relatives; see which of them works for a firm with overseas connections. Often a bank or a law firm will have contacts you can use.

Get a copy of the international *Herald Tribune* and read the classifieds, locate foreign newspapers (most large cities will have newsstands that carry international newspapers and magazines) and periodicals, or professional journals, for news about what's going on. Check with trade associations for their overseas affiliates. Call consulates or trade offices for information.

TARGETING TOMORROW'S JOB

We live in a society which has changed more in your own lifetime than in the two previous centuries; a society which is caught up in an apparently irreversible cycle of problem followed by solution, followed by bigger problems which grow out of earlier solutions. It is a world where change is substituted for progress, and growth replaces contribution as the major life force. You are in the middle of a technological tornado which is burning up its center at an almost incomprehensible rate.

And, according to the Department of Health, Education, and Welfare, if you have recently entered the workforce, you will probably have four or five careers in your worklife. Start now to target them.

As far as we can see, there are only three approaches available for playing the job game:

1. You can resign yourself to whatever the workworld brings you, and attempt to gain as many material rewards as possible to numb yourself into a feeling that, somehow, you made it.

2. You can expand the full recognition of yourself and realize that it is not the position that's important, but the way you hold it—the position about the position. An enlightened context for your life which, indeed, does work.

3. You can realize that you are responsible for the worklife you end up with, and the satisfaction it holds, and identify the dynamic relationship which will allow you to continually express yourself into the workforce in a way which produces satisfaction. Strategy 3, of course, is what this book is about. With some assistance from strategy 2.

With a reasonably well-thought-out program you can easily identify target areas which represent the next generation of hot jobs, those which wield economic power and prestige and are in the mainstream of the world game. All you need to do is, literally, open your eyes and see what's coming down the pike, and then, by identifying the growth pattern, select or *create* the kind of job targets which will be appropriate to the directions you see. All it takes is a little confidence in the obvious.

TACTIC #22

Visit your local library. Ask the librarian to put you in touch with some references or articles which discuss the development of industry and business. Look through an index of articles in Business Week, Fortune, or the Wall Street Journal. Alternatively, call a trade association and ask what articles they recommend in your field.

COMPLETION CHECK ☐

You can create a job by identifying an obvious future trend, seeing how this trend relates to what you have been doing and to your interests and skills, adding whatever education and/or training you need, and communicating this to the right person:

"Ms. Frisk, I was looking at your plans to erect that new microwave transmission network, and I wonder if you are aware of some of the new laser beam techniques which could cut transmission costs by 40%."

Or:

"Ms. Pulling, I have an idea how you could bring more people into your training seminars. I think that we could establish connections with local industry, and probably bring in 25 to 30 new people per month, I could assist you in setting this up."

Job creation is simply advanced problem solving. You don't have to be a genius, and you aren't required to be able to see what's happening two decades down the line—two years is more than enough.

Jan Johnson

After hanging around the house for years convincing myself that I was really not equipped for anything in this world other than raising kids, taking care of a house, and, from time to time, playing secretary, I actually went out and created a career for myself. A career that gives me what I want, feeds my ego, lets me talk to people more than 12 years old, and also pays me now, after six years, $18,000 per year. Here's how it happened:

In college I took some prelaw courses and some credits in business. I had this vague idea of going to law school, but at that time there weren't as many women doing that as there are now, and my family really didn't support the idea. So instead, I got a job in a small law firm in Crescent City as a legal secretary.

It started well. I was single, and got to meet people and go out a lot, so I could forget the tedium of typing legal briefs and depositions all day long. I can't believe that some women actually do that day in day out, week after weary week, year after year. I'd rather be a housewife. Which is exactly what I became when I married one of our clients. That, of course, was the end of my career at that law firm.

I had Jamie a year and a half later, and decided to stay home a few years, which stretched into seven before I even knew it. I broke out of my rut after I joined a women's group. I wasn't a strident feminist, but some of my friends were going, and I joined them.

One day a woman spoke to us about jobs, and the legal movement to bring women and other people into jobs that they had previously been excluded from. I was intrigued.

My friend Bev and I got very interested in the area of equal opportunity. At first, we were concerned about how it applied to us, but then we began to realize that with the government pressure escalating, companies would be very interested in learning how to stay out of trouble and, since the whole equal employment opportunity thing was only a few years old, there weren't many people around who knew what was going on. It was a natural, and tied right in to my earlier interest in law.

Bev and I spent three months learning about it together. We read every article we could dig up. We contacted the National Organization of Women, and got some stuff from them. We went to Washington for a solid week, visited the EEOC, read and made copies of the legislation and hearings, and got a strong sense of the direction that things were moving.

Our most productive step was to call a woman we had read about. She was doing some consulting with AT&T, which had already had some EEO problems. Martha met us for lunch twice, let us sit in on some meetings she was running, and gave us the names of some of the people we should contact.

Once we got over our fear of the phone, we each made up a list of 25 corporations in our area that we would be willing to work for and called them up. I would suggest to the personnel manager that we should get together and talk about what they were doing in the EEO area, and how I could possibly help them. I got to actually meet with 12 companies, and got job offers from four. I could have gotten three more if I pushed. I took a job with Consolidated Refineries as EEO specialist. I've changed jobs twice since then, and am now personnel manager of a retailing chain, and love it. I know now that all it takes to find a good job is to stay in touch with what's going on in the world.

TACTIC #23

Get on the telephone, call the personnel managers of a couple of firms in the area of your job target interest. Ask them to tell you how they see their long-term openings shaping up. What kinds of people are they expecting to need in the next year or so? What skills are the hardest for them to locate? Don't push for a specific job, just more information and experience on the phone.

COMPLETION CHECK ☐

YOUR CRYSTAL BALL

You are living in the middle of an information complex, and probably everything you need to know about areas of future job development and growth is at your fingertips if you are willing to dig it out. Are you willing? Or are you still stuck in the traditional point of view that the job you get, the work you do, is pretty much something that someone else—the placement counselor at school, the employment agent, your family, the newspaper classifieds—handles for you?

It's hard to break old patterns, and this "Show me where I report" attitude about work is one of the oldest. We aren't trained to look upon work as an opportunity for creative expression. Most of us are never shown how to use the resources at hand to open up new careers for ourselves. There *are* resources which will provide you with information on what's happening. Here are three to start with now:

Business publications like *Business Week, Wall Street Journal, Forbes, Barrons, Fortune*
Professional societies in your target area
Trade publications in your field

AFFIRMATIONS

Repeat:
I am not my job title.
I am willing to relate to work in a way which reflects my own internal satisfaction and joy of life.

I am able and skilled, and willing to use my abilities to create value in the world in the best way that I can.

I am willing to uncover specific job targets which reflect my skills and abilities, and to undertake the job search only after I have become clear about these.

Once I have selected my job targets I am willing to do what's necessary to achieve them.

Now go back over these affirmations again, and this time make them even more real for yourself. Stop at each one and see if it is true for you.

Are you really willing? If you encounter resistance along the way will you continue to press? How long?

It's easy to agree with the statements, but quite another thing to experience them in living terms. The traditional thinking is generally in a counter direction:

> "I am best described by my job title."
>
> "Like it or not, you've got to work."
>
> "I hate the work, but it pays well."
>
> "I'm looking for a job—do you have anything?"
>
> "The job market is tough. You're lucky to find any job."

This negativism is an integral part of our education for work. You find it reinforced at every turn, by parents, teachers, newspapers, even many career counselors and consultants.

The consciousness that work is something you *do* with your life, not something you "*get*," is a recent phenomenon. But the new awareness won't have any value for you if you simply "believe" it just because we say so. You've got to look more deeply within to see if you are willing to create the truth for yourself. Are you?

TARGETS

A target is a statement of your intention and willingness. It is not a hope. It is not a dream. It is a reality which has yet to be formalized.

TARGETING

The only way to effectively approach job targets is to imagine yourself at the final objective, and then identify all the apparent obstacles between you and success. See the obstacles as the steps you need to take to actualize the target for yourself. Just include them within the purpose of your objective, and notice that they actually support you in getting what you want, by pointing up the next thing that needs to be done.

Objection from you:

It sounds like double-talk. I don't understand how the obstacles to the target are actually supportive to my achieving it. It's a semantic trick. Frankly, I don't know if I can accomplish my target at all, and I'm not willing to buy this theoretical positive thinking stuff. I'll do the best I can: I'll try to make my targets but I won't guarantee that I'll do it.

Response from us:

Thanks for being honest. Most people never really target for anything. They pretend to really want something, then get "determined," and "try" to make it. And their point of view is essentially that they won't make it unless they are lucky. *People don't achieve their targets, because they allow the obstacles to become reasons for not making it.* If you are not willing to take absolute responsibility for the results of a particular target, then change your target to something you *would* be willing to achieve. Don't set yourself up to be a loser in your own terms.

Your rebuttal:

You mean that I should pick an easy target, so that I will be sure that I can make it. What good is that?

Our reply:

No. Every target which you set for yourself should be an expression of your willingness to be uncomfortable. If it does not require some effort or some confrontation, it isn't a valuable target. All real growth or movement is accompanied by a feeling of uncomfortableness and challenge. Think of the first race you ran, the first big date, the first time you made a speech, acted in a play, or disagreed with a popular opinion. The other side of being uncomfortable is accomplishment.

Select job targets which you know will produce some discomfort and challenge and be willing to handle everything which comes up along the way. If you do that, you will achieve your targets.

TACTIC #24

Go back to the list of potential job targets you were left with when you completed Tactic No. 18. Rank them in order of interest to you. Then select the top four as your job targets—with the understanding that you are willing to do what's necessary to get one of these positions.

Write each of the top four on a separate sheet in your notebook, and then list all the things you can think of which could get in the way of your achieving this target. After you have listed all the obstacles, go back and write down the things you would have to do to overcome the obstacles.

COMPLETION CHECK [ ]

FREE LANCE

Geraldine Newton

The first people to get fired are in public relations. At the merest hint of the economic sniffles, out they go. I mean, why not—the client isn't all that excited about what we do when everything is rosy, so what the hell do they need us around when they're chopping the budget? It's a fickle career. I know some fine publicity people who have probably put In more time behind the wheel of a taxi than behind a typewriter.

TARGETING

A few years ago things got so bad where I worked that the whole agency folded. It was a very sobering situation.

I decided that this time, whatever I did, I wasn't going to be back at the same old game. Very brave, but what to do? The idea of changing careers gave me this hot sinking feeling in my stomach. I spent this one very spacy weekend by myself. Very sad, very thoughtful, playing out my life over and over. Real thoughts of failure, frustration, and regret that I hadn't picked a different field, or had stayed married. Lots of stuff like that.

Anyway, I came through with flying colors. I came up with the idea of going into free-lance public relations. To build up my own clients on small jobs or projects. At first, I thought it was a crazy idea. I wanted security, and here I was going out on a limb.

I knew that one of the things I had to do was to improve my ability to communicate, to let people know I could do the job. I did TM, which really calmed me. And then I did the *est* training. It was fabulous. I got in touch with the idea that whatever I wanted I could get if I was willing to play from a position of responsibility. That I could be responsible for my own worklife.

I contacted everyone I knew personally in the business—clients, media people, and other people in PR firms. In a short time I picked up three small accounts, which at least paid the rent. This gave me the courage to make my new career exactly the way I wanted it. I decided to represent authors who had just published books, and who felt that they weren't being actively enough represented by their publishers. I had a package deal in which I charged them $1500 for four months plus expenses. I now have around ten clients at any one time, the product of an initial phone campaign to publishers and friends, and lots of follow-up. I love it, and I have more security, since I can go out and get a new client whenever I lose one, and I make more money than I ever made before. And I have more fun. The only security you have is inside yourself.

There are scores of work areas in which it is an accepted and established modus operandi to provide your services on an hourly or daily or project basis. And as we break our traditional attachment to the nine-to-five work routine the number of areas which open up for free lancing will continue to expand.

You are a free lancer when you have clearly dedicated yourself to the full-time project of providing your skills on a part-time basis to a variety of clients, and are responsible for soliciting your own assignments and billing them directly.

At a higher-paid, more expert level, the same work style is called consulting. Some of the more recognized areas of freelance work are:

Writing	Advertising	Public relations
Editing	Casting	Talent manager
Research	Gardening	Artist's representative
Illustrating	Bartender	
Decorating	Catering	Tour guide
Bookkeeping	Plant care	Translator
Accounting	Costume designing	Real estate agent
Nursing		
Designing	Typist	Child care
Landscaping	Masseuse	Shopper
Architecture	Music teacher	Programmer
Carpentry	Photographer	Systems anaylst
Specialized engineering	Filmmaker Stylist	—and about 100 more.

This is the beginning of the list. You can take it from there. The essence of free-lance work is that you are responsible for developing your own customers or clients. It can be done by small ads in local newspapers, notices on community bulletin boards, direct solicitation by phone or mail, and most importantly, by word of mouth. Satisfied clients tell others.

If you are shy or embarrassed about letting people know how good you are, or billing well for your time, then free lance might turn into part-time starvation for you. A rule of thumb for charging for your time is to bill two or three times what you would get if you were working for a salary. This will compensate for the lack of fringe benefits, and for your downtime when you are developing new business. As your own boss you face a major management problem: how to keep you, the employee, at work. As a beginning free lancer you need to set up a weekly and daily schedule of specific things to do to let the right people know what you can do for them. Even though you are booked up with work, you need to continue to develop new leads and contacts for the future.

YOUR OWN SHOW

The quest for fame and fortune lures over 500,000 would-be entrepreneurs into starting their own businesses each year, according to the Small Business Administration, the federal agency responsible for policies and programs to aid and help finance small businesses. Unfortunately, as divorce frequently follows marriage, business failures provide a sobering view of the other side of the entrepreneurial dream.

According to the Dun & Bradstreet Business Failure Record published for 1975, the most common causes of bankruptcies are incompetence, undercapitalization, unbalanced experience, lack of experience in the line, and lack of managerial experience.

Having your own business is an exciting and frequently rewarding and remunerative approach to your worklife; one which can motivate you for many, many years. It can also hold much pain, frustration, hard work, and low return. It is almost always an adventure. There are five essentials that must be met in starting your own profitable business:

1. A product or service which produces substantially more value for the customer than it costs, which can be produced or delivered for significantly less than it sells for.

2. A conscious, tested way to communicate this value to potential customers in a way which cost-effectively creates sales.

3. A management or manager willing to set up and observe objective criteria for measuring performance

against a predetermined plan, and to let go of ideas which demonstrably aren't working.

4. An organized, clear, time-oriented, truthful business plan which sets out specific goals and timetables, and an accurate realistic budget reviewed by an accountant.

5. Enough money to carry you through your business plan even if 50% of your goals are not met on time.

If any of these essential conditions are not met, think seriously about holding off until they are. If you have prepared yourself carefully, go to it, and play the game outrageously. Keep looking for the things which produce value for others and move in that direction. Do what works and drop what doesn't work.

Be willing to try again if the first time around doesn't produce the results you are looking for. In a TV interview a few years ago, David Susskind interviewed four men who had each made a million dollars before they were 35. Among the four, they had been involved in something like 75 different ventures, businesses, jobs, or other activities before they made their fortunes.

MOVING ON

By this time, if you are following this book responsibly, doing the exercises, and keeping your workbook, you should be clear about four specific job targets which you can *own*, that is, which you can get behind and be responsible for. Using the tactics in the remaining pages, you will be able to achieve them. Really. It's that powerful.

If you have been willing to do the exercises and tactics, and to confront your resistance and excuses, terrific! Take out some time to acknowledge yourself, pat yourself on the back, have a beer. Have two beers. You have accomplished what many others have excused away or have not found time or space to go through.

If you are feeling guilty right now, you know you haven't done your homework. You've probably put together a few justifications like "I'll do it later," or "I already know that," or "Who has the time for that kind of stuff? I'm looking for a job, not a dedication." Or

TARGETING

perhaps you have some other ideas that have kept you skimming rather than digging into the material in this book.

We hope that after you've scanned through the book looking for quick fixes, you will return to examine some of the basic personal issues raised in these pages. We continue to support your search for a more meaningful connection to your worklife. *If you can, before moving on, go back and complete any of the exercises or tactics which you've skipped. It will work better.*

If you're not up to looking back right now, just make a note of that. Move on, and please help yourself to whatever you can use.

REMINDERS AND REFERENCES

Reminders

- Work is not something you get; it is something you do.
- Fully 85% of the jobs available on any given day are not advertised.
- Remember, you can use the phone to start collecting *information* from people in your field of interest. Find out the facts from people who are daily on the line. Make the job area *real* for yourself.

References

I've Had It: A Practical Guide to Moving Abroad by Robert Hopkins. Holt, Rinehart, Winston, New York.

A Business of Your Own: Franchise Opportunities, Drake Publishers, New York.

You, Inc. A Detailed Escape Route to Being Your Own Boss by Peter Weaver. Doubleday, New York, 1975.

On Your Own: 99 Alternatives to a 9 to 5 Job by Kathy Matthews. Vintage Books, Random House, New York, 1977.

Question: Do you have a job target(s)? What is it?

5

WORK EDUCATION

NEW EDUCATION AND TRAINING

Listen to Alvin Toffler about education:

"What passes for education today, even in our 'best' schools and colleges, is a hopeless anachronism. Parents look to education to fit their children for life in the future. Teachers warn that lack of an education will cripple a child's chances in the world of tomorrow.

"Yet for all this rhetoric about the future, our schools face backward toward a dying system, rather than forward to the emerging new society . . . in a system which will be dead before they are."

Amen.

We are bloated with an educational system which, with few exceptions, does not prepare students to meet the direct challenges of their world. Students are swept downstream from course to course, year to year, amassing $20-30-50,000 worth of certificates, diplomas, degrees, and then find themselves out on the streets without an idea of what their work will be, or how to go about attaining it. Mass education is a failure when it comes to creating the context for a satisfying life's work.

However, once you have created your work goals, your knowledge of the system through which education and skills training are delivered can make a major contribution to your life. When you use education as a tool to support your life goals, the experience brightens considerably. When you know what it is that you need to learn in order to get what you want, a school or training course seems a natural place to be, and the material to be learned goes down like soup to the hungry.

As you develop long-term and short-term job targets you will see areas where additional training or education is called for. Using good location techniques and references, it will be a snap to find out where to pick up the new skills you need for virtually any job area. In focusing on your education, always start with job targets first, and then find out with certainty what skills are required. Don't allow yourself to be talked into getting a master's degree in French if all you need to be able to do is communicate with your Paris office. As we have discussed earlier, a college degree may be at least a technical necessity for many fields. If you don't have one, see if you can work out a plan to obtain it with a minimal disruption of your work agenda. If you go to college full time, work out a way to stay in touch with a job target and employer along the way—through summer and vacation work, co-op programs (part work, part school), or other means.

Here are some sources of education and training information to help you prepare for your first job, or to rise through the ranks toward your ultimate target.

ON-THE-JOB TRAINING

A very practical way to build your skills is to look for training opportunities in and around any job you have. Possibilities abound in almost every job area for you to expand your skills along with holding down a job. If you are a receptionist, pick up or improve your typing skills. If you are a typist, learn steno, or programming. If you are a secretary, learn bookkeeping and about word processing machines. If you are a programmer, learn systems work. If you are in personnel, go nights for your M.B.A. If you are a media planner, learn more about account management. If you are an account executive, learn more about creative. If you are a copywriter, learn more about merchandising. If you are an attorney, learn accounting. If you are a teacher, develop your writing skills. If you are a writer, learn typing.

The old adage still applies: *Earn while you learn. Or is it learn while you earn?*

HOW TO DO IT

There is a massive crop of how-to-do-it books available in your local bookstore, drugstore, supermarket, or library. Most of these books will not make you an expert. They will, however, give you a good introductory sense of the subject—a kind of preknowledge which will at least make you more comfortable with the subject, able to talk about it, and will frequently give you references to more serious works. Ask practitioners in the field for the names of books they have found helpful.

PROFESSIONAL CLASS

Trade and professional societies abound. You can find a national organization dedicated to everything from the preservation of wildflowers to the expansion of hot-air ballooning. These self-interest groups usually have staffs of people who know what's going on in the field and can give you references to books and courses. Some offer career placement services.

You can find the names and addresses of associations in your field by going to the library and referring to *The Encyclopedia of Associations*. Check with your librarian for further sources of information. When you have identified an organization in your field, check the phone directory to see if they have a local chapter. Make contact by phone—you'll get more information faster than by mail.

YOUR LOCAL LIBRARY

When was the last time you stopped in at your local library? Well, if you're interested in finding out more about any particular job target area, a stop at the library is mandatory.

Books, periodicals, reference works, and bibliographies will give you direction and insight toward your job target field.

TACTIC #25

> Plan to spend a few hours in the business or reference section of your local library, or at a university library. Telephone a school or library and describe what types of information you are seeking, and ask what branch or location would be most appropriate for you.
>
> Go to the library with a list of your specific job targets. Look for textbooks, magazine articles, trade and professional associations, directories, etc. Other books on job-finding techniques may be available.
>
> COMPLETION CHECK ☐

THE TRADE SCHOOL

There are over 7500 private trade and technical schools in the U.S., specializing in occupations which don't require a college education—from electronic techniques to truckdriver to dental hygienist to disk jockey. Select one carefully after a personal visit and a call to the local Better Business Bureau. Contact a potential employer and ask if the school has a good reputation in the field. Most schools are professionally run, provide a good education, and will negotiate a very fair contract. The ones which make the news are poorly run, sell hard, and often push careers in which there may not be much of a future, or in which education can be obtained more effectively elsewhere. (Schools promising stewardess careers, for example, frequently are not recognized by the airlines, which do their own training.)

As we've said, always select your job target first, based upon your own interest and skills and job market information, then look for the school. You can obtain a directory of private trade and technical schools by writing to the National Association of Trade and Technical Schools.

THE MIDNIGHT OIL

Home study courses are available for almost every possible subject, discipline, vocation, occupation, or fantasy. Don't take this route unless you are *fully motivated*. Many start, few complete. It takes fortitude and good eyesight to learn complex subjects through the mails. But there are valuable courses available which can give you much of the technical knowledge you need in many fields. You can find out more by writing to the National Home Study School Council.

APPRENTICESHIP TRAINING

There are about half a million paid apprenticeships available through unions and nonunion shops, primarily to younger members of our workforce who are willing to work hard for a minimal wage. Apprenticeships are the most direct and practical way to enter many crafts and skilled trades.

More than 300 job areas can be reached through the apprenticeship route, from aviation technician and bookbinder to carpenter and upholsterer. If you are interested, contact the local office of your state employment service.

COOPERATIVE WORK-STUDY PROGRAMS

One of the most practical and rewarding ways to get an education while furthering career goals is to locate one of the no-nonsense work-study programs available at many reality-minded colleges. Usually the programs are set up so that you report to work with a cooperating employer for a portion of the year, then play student for the remaining time. You get paid for your work time by the employer, while you develop vocational skills which put you ahead of full-time students in terms of familiarity and understanding of the work process.

Co-op programs are developed in close coordination with school officials and employers, and will be strongest in the more traditional work areas.

COMMUNITY COLLEGES

The public two-year community college is one of the fastest-growing segments of the education universe. Most such colleges offer well-focused, practical programs with a high reality quotient, and a strong relationship to career growth and development. Often these schools have effective career counseling and placement departments, in keeping with their orientation toward a stronger relationship between school and work. Community colleges in general have strong ties with the local community; they may have facilities for aptitude testing and counseling open to community residents who are not matriculated in the school.

ADULT EDUCATION

Your work experience is a lifetime affair, like it or not. It can be a constantly growing, expanding relationship, or you can find yourself repeating the same routines year after year, getting progressively more bitter as you wait out the final years of your career.

Visit any organization for a while and you will begin to notice the people whose careers have leveled off. They look up to engage you in idle conversation each time you pass, start cleaning up to go home 20 minutes before the end of the workday, and are very willing to tell you how screwed up the organization is. They have allowed themselves to stop growing. They are now living for weekends and vacation time.

COMPLAINT

Well what else can I do? They won't promote a person around this place unless you kiss a lot of asses along the way. Sure, you'll get your 8% raise every year. Big deal. Doesn't even match the cost of living. Yes, I'd like to have more responsibility, but management around here plays favorites. They promoted that young black girl right over my head. I wouldn't want to look into *that* promotion too closely! They said it was because she learned how to operate the new minicomputer system, went to school and all that. How's a person supposed to go to school 3 nights a week and raise a family too? If you ask me, her promotion doesn't have anything to do with that. Well, they can do what they want with their computers. I'll mind my own business and get my job done, and that's all they need to know about me.

Sour grapes are a product of sitting too long in the same place. If you don't continue to expand your skills, you will definitely reach a level where you are stuck. An ongoing increase of your skills, abilities, and interests is almost a guarantee of expanded work satisfaction and pleasure. More work satisfaction and a bigger paycheck grow out of your ability to solve more problems, and your ability to solve more problems expands as you acquire more tools—more knowledge and skills.

There are exciting adult education programs in almost every city in this country, and you can pick up new and diverse skills for pleasure and for profit.

Contact your local board of education, community college, or four-year college. Find out what they have to offer, and what other programs they can tell you about.

Keep learning. Keep earning.

TACTIC #26

List your most recent job or jobs, or your job targets at an entry level. Below, list an expanded position you would like to be in three years from now, and below that a five-year goal.

To the right of these listings, write down some of the specific skills you feel you would need to acquire, to make your three- or five-year jumps. Then, on the far right-hand side, list where you think you can obtain the training or skills listed.

COMPLETION CHECK ☐

REMINDERS AND REFERENCES

Reminder

- Using education as a tool to support *your own* life goals is an entirely different experience from getting educated to do something that someone else wants you to do.

WORK EDUCATION

References

Finding Facts Fast: How to Find Out What You Want to Know Immediately by Alden Todd. William Morrow & Co., Inc., New York, 1972.

Go Hire Yourself an Employer by Richard Irish. Doubleday, Garden City, N.Y., 1973.

The Guide to Career Education by Muriel Lederer. Quadrangle, New York, 1976.

Catalogue of Business & Vocational Educational Materials. Thompson–Mitchell & Associates, 2996 Grandview Ave., N.E., Roberts Building, Atlanta, Georgia 30305.

Other Resources

For apprenticeship training, write to:
 Bureau of Apprenticeship Training
 U.S. Department of Labor
 Washington, D.C. 20210

For schools offering Co-Op programs:
 Cooperative Education Association
 Drexel University
 Philadelphia, Pa. 19104

For free directory of trade and technical schools:
 National Association of Trade & Technical Schools
 2121 L St., N.W.
 Washington, D.C. 20009

For information on home-study courses:
 National Home Study School Council
 1001 18th St., N.W.
 Washington, D.C. 20009

6

INSIDE THE HIDDEN JOB MARKET

Everybody knows what to do when you are looking for a job. You get the help wanted section of your largest local newspaper, pour a cup of coffee, sit down at the kitchen table, pen in hand, and circle the advertised jobs which seem to fit your idea of yourself and what you are looking for.

If you've ever looked for a job, you are familiar with your own version of the scene: the hope that you will find exactly what you are looking for, the mystery about some of the listings, the obscurity of many of the terms, the disappointment over jobs which seem just right but require more education, or moving, and the frustration of knowing that thousands of other job seekers are pouring over the same newsprint, copying down the same names and addresses, mailing résumés to the same box numbers. The futility of it all!

This repetitious, passive, and unimaginative approach to your future worklife makes you feel powerless. But what to do, where to go, who are the right people, the right jobs? How do you get out of this rut? *HELP!*

Help is on the way. Put down your ballpoints, fold up your newspapers, gather around, and listen to the secrets of the Hidden Job Market: a treasure trove of jobs that haven't been advertised yet, but are very real —and, in many cases, are just what you are looking for. In this chapter we will show you how to locate specific unadvertised positions which fit the job targets you have selected. But first let's back up and look at the system by which jobs are created and filled.

THE EMPLOYMENT PROCESS

We want you to expand your thinking about jobs, what they are, and where they come from. How it happens that Bruce Kirkland calls personnel one

INSIDE THE HIDDEN JOB MARKET 111

Monday morning and asks them to help him find three new researchers, or why, after months of no employment advertising, IBM suddenly runs a full-page ad in the *New York Times* for a variety of technical talent.

If you know how the employment process works, you will be able to discover openings long before they become public record.

What creates job openings? Almost any productive business activity does. For example:

Increased business demand
New products
New social problems
New inventions
Legislation
Environmental challenges
Social trends
Plant relocations
Terminations
Retirement
New management

Literally everything which influences this wild wobbly world of ours is reflected in the workworld.

If we discover that the Russians and the Mafia are monitoring our microwave communications system, within months 50 newly hired communications engineers are working on the problem. When a craze like skateboarding takes hold in upper Minnesota and receives national media exposure, stand back. Within six months there are dozen of small firms designing, manufacturing, promoting, and selling skateboards, and 1500 people are employed in a new industry.

Virtually anything you read about in the morning paper has influenced someone's job by the time you sit down to dinner that night. There is virtually no difference between this daily soap opera we call life and the workworld. They are just different perceptions of the same thing. WORK IS LIFE. It isn't just today's classifieds.

TACTIC #27

Get a copy of a newspaper from a city or community in which you would like to live and work.

Pick five articles or news items in this paper, and make a list of all the ways the job market could be influenced by the event or situation written about. What new jobs could be created, and in what field. Do the same thing for a publication like the Wall Street Journal, or a whole issue of Time magazine.

Continue to follow this process with all of your reading and observation of events in the world around you.

COMPLETION CHECK ☐

Just as boxes on the market shelves reveal very little about the creation, testing, manufacture, and promoting of new products, help wanted advertisements tell next to nothing about the hiring process. These ads are the final step in a sometimes long and involved series of events which you should know about. Tune in to the real lifework story of Hensley Capehart and his associate, Suzie.

Hensley Capehart

Although Suzie lacked experience, I liked her. She had a terrific personality, looked good, and paid attention when I talked or gave instructions. I thought it was just a matter of some training. Looking back, I see that when I interviewed her I pretty much gave the job away. I didn't really probe to see if she had what it took to do the work.

Anyhow, her job was to put together a number of reports, graphs, and statistics which would reflect how well our division was doing. We would feed her all the production and sales figures and she would play around with them and give us pictures of how we were doing for different months in different regions. Stuff like that.

There was one major report she had to put out which was supposed to be in my boss's hands by the tenth of each month, which means that I needed it by the eighth. It was the most important part of her job, since we would read sales programs, inventory, and hiring plans right out of the information in this report.

The first three or four reports she did were fine. She was helped by the woman whose job she had taken, who was now in another department.

(January) In January I didn't get the report on time. When I finally received it, it was four days late, and had a few errors which took a day to correct.

(February) The next month's report was also late, and had some errors which, frankly, I also missed, but which my boss was quick to point out. I was beginning to get worried.

(April) The March and April reports made it on time, but were not organized according to the form we had decided upon. They didn't look good, but I passed them through rather than delay them. This is when I had my first serious talk with Susan. I told her that she would have to do a better job. As I told her I saw this glassy defiant look come over her eyes, and I knew inside that the end was near. But I didn't really face it realistically.

(June) June was the last straw. Suzie was out sick on the day I should have had her report, and when I found it on her desk in rough form, I saw how confusing the whole thing was to her. It took us two full days to piece it together. Late again. For the last time, I vowed.

(July) It took me three weeks to tell Suzie that I was going to replace her in the job. I never have been very good at firing people. I know I'm too much of a nice guy, but I don't like to put a person through that. I gave her one month's notice on condition that she work with me on the next report to make sure I knew all of the steps. The first thing I did was to put out the word in our department that we were in the market for a new analyst. I also dug out the applications from the past Fall when we had last interviewed. I told a few of my friends, and posted the position.

(August) By the middle of August I had three

interviews, and was interested in one person. I invited him back for a second interview, but he couldn't do it right away because he was leaving for a vacation trip. I decided to wait, and did the report myself, since Suzie was gone.

(September) I interviewed a few more people from the files, and the guy who had been on vacation still looked good, so I made him an offer. He thought about it for two weeks, and then surprised me by turning it down. I was really in a bind now, and damn tired of doing these reports myself, so I called personnel.

(October) Last week personnel ran an ad and today we are swamped. We've gotten 150 responses, and more arrive every day. This doesn't count the phone calls which my secretary has fielded for me. We've turned the whole thing over to personnel now, and they will do the initial screening. They should start sending me people to interview in about a week. I can't believe how long this whole thing has taken.

MAKING CONTACT AHEAD OF THE PACK

It will normally take anywhere from six weeks to six months or longer for an organization to go from the realization of a need to actually advertising for the position. Most of the time they will have filled the position from within, or from an employee referral, or with someone's friend. This is true of a replacement, or for a situation where the organization is planning to expand, diversify, or move in a different direction.

Jobs exist as needs to be filled long before they show up in classifieds. As a matter of fact, *something like 85% of the job openings or employment needs which exist on a given day are not advertised in public media.* This is an important piece of information for you as a job seeker, because if you can make contact with potential employers before the jobs get advertised, you have the field to yourself. In the case of Hensley Capehart, for example, you can see that if you had been a competent report writer and had made personal contact with him in April or May, or any time before the ad

INSIDE THE HIDDEN JOB MARKET   115

ran, you would have certainly had an interview, and if you had made a favorable impression, you could have had the job without any competition. Homer didn't want to go through all that aggravation!

"*Hold it,*" you say. "How do I know who to contact, and when they have an opening?" A very astute question. Stay right here for the unfolding of the answer.

TURNOVER

Most organizations experience turnover (people who quit or are terminated) at the rate of 20 to 25% per year. When you add in people who change jobs within the firm, the change rate climbs to between 30 and 40%. *On the average, jobs change once every three years.* Add to this the fact that organizations tend to expand and you will begin to get the idea we want to hammer home:

With turnover and expansion constant throughout the job world, and with most employers knowing about and planning for upcoming job changes well in advance, the employment picture is not static, but an ongoing flow of opportunity into which an informed and assertive job seeker can selectively insert her (him) self at virtually any time.

BUT HOW DO I DO IT?
Keep reading and stay awake.

NUMBERS GAME

For example, you are job-targeted as a graphic designer with a particular skill and interest in boating, and you surmise that the top 20 firms in the field (boat manufacturers, outboard manufacturers, boating suppliers) each have an average of two full-time graphic designers on staff and that these people probably change jobs around once every four years (25% turnover), and that management will generally know about upcoming changes at least 90 days before they turn them over to personnel. What you will be able to conclude is this:

With a total of 40 positions covered, 10 people (25%) will leave or be promoted each year. Because each position will be open for an average of three months, *in any given month* there will be (across the sample group of 20 employers) at least two projected, unadvertised openings with this job target.

If you are not clear about this, please go back and reread the figures.

CONCLUSION FOR YOU TO GET

You can create an important advantage for yourself in your job target fields if you are willing to identify prospective employers, not on the basis of employment ads, but from the premise that if you contact enough of the right people in the right firms you will uncover opportunities that are not public knowledge, and may never be.

TACTIC #28

Pick one or more of your job targets, and call someone you know of in the field, or call the trade association. Ask them if they know what the general turnover rate in the field is, or if they don't know, ask how you can find out. You might call the personnel departments of several employers (although they are often unwilling to admit to high turnover).

COMPLETION CHECK ☐

FEAR OF TRYING

It will come as no surprise to you by now to hear that people generally have a lot of resistance to being in the job market or changing careers or, for that matter, starting out in any new personal direction. The easy way is the popular way. The shortest route to a job—the one with the least effort and personal confrontation—is the way that most people take. And, as we have said, people don't "own" their jobs. They are there, frequently, because they *have* to be there. They are stuck with a lingering sense that, somehow, if they had looked a little further, not jumped so quickly, expanded their search, not been so eager to get the paycheck, they would have found something more satisfying—more related to the real person.

Job finding and career changing are high on the stress scale. They are human/social transactions which provoke fear and trembling in young and old, rich or poor, man and woman, successful and unsuccessful. Normally secure people become needy, sad, worried, and inert. Business planners who can map out corporate plans years in advance approach their own job campaign on a day-to-day basis, and wonder why they aren't seeing more results. Nightmares replace daydreams when people find themselves threatened with the possibility of not making it in the job game. Every interview is a potential rejection. Every phone call holds the possibility of a turndown.

UNLESS

Unless you are willing to turn the whole thing into a game.

"Some game," you say. "It's easy for you to feel that way. You're not looking for a job. You probably don't have to worry about your next paycheck, or paying the rent. Frankly, all I want is to get a job that pays well and doesn't hassle me so much."

Yes. We got it. The job search *is* a pain in the tail, it *is* threatening to people, it *is* hard work, *and* it is a game if you are willing to play it rather than struggle at it. The thing that makes it heavy is the point of view that jobs are scarce, and that if you are turned down at any stage it is an invalidation of you personally. But both of these are lies. There is no scarcity of job opportunity and most turndowns are simply part of the process. Let's examine the fallacies.

SCARCITY

As one experienced employment counselor expressed it recently: "When someone asks me what the unemployment rate is, I ask him back, 'Are you working?' If he says 'Yes,' I tell him that the unemployment rate is zero. If he isn't working, then I tell him that he's faced with 100% unemployment."

Unemployment or employment figures are irrelevant as measures of your own situation or of what you should do about it. As we expressed earlier, most people rarely look beyond the positions which are advertised in the public job market. When they don't find just what they are looking for, jobs are scarce. When they respond to an ad and find that there are 100 other applicants, jobs are scarce. The real truth:

- The U.S. job market has been expanding at the rate of over 3 million new jobs each year.
- Several million people retire from the labor force every year.
- Even with a minimum turnover rate of 20%, an additional 19,600,000 people change jobs each year.
- With the explosive growth of social, cultural, political, and resource-oriented problems, and the ongoing technological expansion, the range of personal opportunity is expanding daily.
- With a clear sense of your own skills and abilities and the techniques in this book, you can literally create job opportunities for yourself which not only pay you a competitive wage, but also provide you with a solid basis of personal satisfaction which is priceless.

TURNDOWNS

This may be the most valuable part of the book for you.

Every job campaign looks like this:
NO NO NO NO NO NO NO NO
NO NO NO NO NO NO NO NO
NO NO NO NO NO NO NO *YES*

INSIDE THE HIDDEN JOB MARKET

If you are a middle-level manager changing careers your job campaign looks like this:
NO NO NO NO NO NO NO NO
NO NO NO NO NO NO NO NO
NO NO NO NO NO NO NO *YES*

If your are a housewife entering the job market for the first time, your job campaign looks like this:
NO NO NO NO NO NO NO NO
NO NO NO NO NO NO NO NO
NO NO NO NO NO NO NO *YES*

If you are a blue-collar worker changing from the construction industry to automotive repair your job campaign looks like this:
NO NO NO NO NO NO NO NO
NO NO NO NO NO NO NO NO
NO NO NO NO NO NO NO *YES*

Every job campaign will be a long series of NOs followed by a *YES*. That is the usual, standard, universal job campaign. And the more willing you are to explore new fields and directions, the more nos you will create. The problem is that most of us see a turndown as a personal rejection, and are so determined to avoid the nos that we get stopped between them. We slow down our job campaign to avoid what we see as inherent rejection. So, by resisting the inevitable turndowns, we stretch out the process.

You need to understand that there is virtually nothing you can do to avoid the series of nos. They are inevitable. Repeat: They are inevitable, there is nothing you can do.

The process of locating a new job—for anyone—entails putting yourself in a number of situations which will result in your being told no. This is not a rejection of you personally, but just a necessary part of the process.

Now for the key:

The best way to approach the job campaign is for you to actually intend to accelerate the number of nos you get. Consciously put yourself out to create nos quickly. Get more turndowns by making more attempts. Make the measure of the speed and effective-

ness of your job campaign the speed and the number of the nos which you receive. You will start getting yeses that much sooner.

You cannot be harmed by turndowns. There are over 400,000 employers in the United States who employ more than 50 workers; in your own job target areas there are probably thousands. Don't be afraid to waste a few dozen by calling and being turned down. There are plenty more where they came from.

TACTIC #29

Get an 8½ x 11 sheet of paper and type, or have typed, ten rows of ten NOs each. Post this over the work area from which you will conduct most of your job campaign. Every time you get a turndown or refusal, however slight, cross off another NO on the sheet. Obtain and cross off at least ten NOs per week.

COMPLETION CHECK ☐

JOB MARKET RESEARCH

Here's where the ante starts to go up, because right in here is where you will have to venture outside the comfort of your home, or mountain retreat, or park bench, and start to interact with the outside world. You know, all those grim-faced people who are just waiting to reject you! (Actually, what you'll meet is probably the gray-haired librarian plus a half-dozen experts who are eager to tell you as much as you want to know about a subject, and then some.)

The purpose of job market research is for you to translate the four job targets you came up with in tactic no. 24 into real flesh-and-blood employers—people who can actually make you an offer you can't refuse. We call these people *employer prospects*.

An employer prospect is an organization or, more accurately, a person within an organization who, you suspect, normally has someone on staff doing the kind of work you are looking for as a job target. While obtaining prospects' names you don't know whether or not they now have an opening or even whether they would normally hire someone in your category. You don't know, but you have a pretty good idea.

Walter Colt

I learned how to do it the hard way. I was a very qualified cameraman, I mean I still am a qualified cameraman, but this time last year, I wasn't quite sure. Two years ago I filmed a documentary which got several awards, and was shown at a prestigious film festival. I thought that would solve my job problems forever, but easy come, easy go, within a year I was unknown from coast to coast.

The way it works in film is that people get to know who you are by what you've done, and when they are putting together a project which is similar they look you up and negotiate a deal. It's the old standby: "Don't call us, we'll call you." It took me six months to realize that the phone wasn't ringing much anymore, and my friends were all asking me what I'd done recently.

My friend Sylvia, who was in the job market for a more regular-type job, dragged me to a career planning seminar at a local community college. I thought it would be very dull, but it gave me some good ideas about my own profession. I decided that I wouldn't wait anymore for fame and fortune to beat a path to my door. I would break all personal precedent, and initiate contacts in places where they could use what I have to offer.

I divided my professional targets into three categories: feature films, documentary and news work, and educational and training films. My first objective was to develop a list of at least 25 potential employers, or producers in each category.

I first contacted the publishers of the basic film trade papers, such as the *American Cinematographer, Hollywood Reporter, Backstage, Theater & Film Casting Weekly, Filmmakers Newsletter,* and a few others. I visited their offices and got permission to read through back issues of their publications, and to look through their membership directories and other reference materials.

I made friends with one of the editors, and after some discussion he was willing to get me a copy of a mailing list of directors and producers that they had for special promotions. This was a real coup, since I recognized several people I had met before, and had forgotten, and a number of other well-known producers. Many were clearly at home addresses, so whatever I sent them would probably get read.

The rest is history. I redid my résumé, created a powerful cover letter to go with it, and had the envelopes and individualized cover letters typed by Sylvia.

I had this idea which, now that I look at it, was very far out: I decided to have a screening of my big film, and pieces of a few industrial things I had done, and invite producers and directors, and corporate training people, to the screenings. My friends said it wouldn't work, that I should just hang around like them, and wait.

I decided to go through with it. I mailed 125 letters and invitations reminding people who I was, and included a good professional résumé. Sylvia and I spent four evenings calling people personally and asking them to come.

We had 38 or 40 people show up on two evenings, and it was really successful. I heard from five people over the next few weeks, and am still working on one of the projects. I know that there is a lot of business which will grow out of this naturally, and I'm thinking about doing it again next year. The breakthrough came when I discovered that it was so easy to dig up the names of the people I wanted to reach. I'm convinced that with a little research and some luck you can find out almost anything.

SOURCES

The first step in your job market research is to identify the specific sources of information which would be applicable to your job targets. The task is to uncover three or four specialized sources, and then to dig into these and pull out the names of potential employers you can contact. After a while you will begin to realize how many possibilities exist for you to explore and exploit.

Here are some of the broad categories of source material easily available and useful in your job campaign:

GENERAL READING

Regular consumer-oriented newsmagazines and newspapers in their routine coverage of the world's happenings often do stories related to a particular growing industry or business, or an area of technological change. As you read through *Time, Newsweek,* and your favorite newspaper, clip out articles or news stories dealing with growth influences in areas you have an interest in. Keep these clipping files up to date as you go through your career, and you will have an ongoing reference of names, organizations, new products, and developments. From the scores of publications available by subscription or at your local newsstand, select those that are most related to your career and life goals and keep in touch with them.

The *New York Times* and the *Wall Street Journal* are national in scope and particularly strong in career-related topics.

BOOKS

There are more books being published now than ever before. Hundreds of new titles are released every week, and your local all-purpose bookstore or library can be a major source of information in virtually any field. Nonfiction titles abound, and you will probably find one or more books about almost any area in which you are interested in working. You won't find specific work references in most books, but you will get information about new trends and directions, and the names of people (including authors) who are expert in the field. People you can contact.

TRADE PUBLICATIONS

Just about every profession, skill area, occupation, hobby, industry, union, discipline, or other cross section of human activity has a magazine or newsletter. These trade publications are probably the most valuable single source for finding out what's going on in a career field. From trade journals and other related publications you can find:

Names of key people
Names of organizations active in the field
New products
New legislation directly or indirectly related to the area
Classified employment ads
Descriptions of new processes or inventions
Business and financial reports

—and, of course, more personal contacts. You can get the names of publications related to any of thousands of topics by looking up the subject area in *Standard Rate & Data*, published by Standard Rate & Data Service. Copies are generally available in advertising agencies, and sometimes in libraries.

TACTIC #30

Locate a copy of Standard Rate & Data, Business Publications, or call and visit an advertising agency and ask for someone in the media department. Look up the topic area of your four job targets, and for each list three or four related publications as sources of information.

COMPLETION CHECK [ ]

BACK ISSUES

By surveying the most recent issues of a trade journal, or by canvassing old newspapers going back as far as a year or two, you can build up a large file of information about potential employers, products, trends, etc. This use of back issues is equivalent to a minieducation in the field.

Some people have had great success contacting employers about last year's or two-year-old job listings. The job was filled 18 months ago, but now the person is being promoted, or he is not working out, or the job is expanding. Certain employers will advertise and fill the same position year after year after year.

---TACTIC #31---

Contact your main local area newspaper, and ask how you can obtain or review back issues of the paper (most keep microfilm files of every issue). Look up several employment sections that are at least a year old, and select ads for openings in your job target areas. Write down at least 15 of these, using as many back issues as necessary.

Then phone the potential hiring authority in each of the advertised firms. Without making reference to the ads, present yourself as a person who can contribute a particular value to the job target area. Keep doing this, and you should be able to average one interview for each eight or ten calls. You can do the same research with trade journals.

COMPLETION CHECK ☐

MEMBERSHIP ASSOCIATIONS

There are as many groups of people organized around a common interest as there are specialized publications. These associations, when directly or indirectly related to one or more of your self-selected job targets, can be a major source of information, direction, and even inspiration in your search for employer prospects. Depending upon their size and purpose, associations can provide you with membership directories (people you can call), publications, booklets about new developments, career information, a resource library, lists of employers in the field, and, frequently, people who will be willing to sit down with you and answer your questions, give you leads, perhaps even steer you to particular employers.

National associations tend to be headquartered in major cities, but many of them have local chapters or affiliates in smaller cities or towns. Check with someone who is in the field, and she/he can probably steer you to the nearest location. A call to the headquarters office will get you membership information and a list of local chapters and/or members. When you have identified the local group, find out when the next meeting is, and see if you can be invited on a trial basis. At the meeting, collect some phone numbers and permission to call the people you meet at a future time for a 30-minute rap session. Once you have met people personally, the doors start to open faster and wider.

SUPER DIRECTORIES

There are three volumes which are unknown to perhaps 80% of the job seekers in the land, and which contain such an immense range of information sources that they can literally turn your job campaign around. These are the *Super Directories*: master references which you can use to pinpoint other materials which are right on target for your job campaign. The super directories do not provide employer leads of their own, but they will lead you to other publications and groups where you can find the specifics you seek. Do whatever you can to locate these directories, and see how much they will expand your job market research, and thus your entire job campaign.

- *Guide to American Directories* contains complete information on over 5200 directories in over 200 subjects.

- *Encyclopedia of Associations* lists over 1200 associations in virtually every field.
- *Standard Rate & Data* has the names and addresses of the trade publications in thousands of fields, listed by topic.

STAND UP AND STRETCH

In our workshops, when we get to the part about job market research and take out the super directories and other information sources, a marked change starts to come over participants who heretofore have been conscious, attentive, and eager to press through personal barriers and resistance. Eyes start to glaze over, one or two people start to nod. The collective consciousness seems to fly out the window and head south.

The thought of going to a library for a few hours to thumb through back copies of trade journals, or to look up employers in directories, reactivates old school images of long boring weekend homework assignments grudgingly pursued while the other kids are outside playing.

We know that right now you would like to look for shortcuts. Ways that you could just make a few phone calls and find out about a terrific job that meets all your standards, and is just down the block. You're tempted to skip this part and move on to résumés and interviews. Anything, as long as you don't have to handle this dull stuff. Right?

We understand. Job market research is like being back in the supply depot when the troops are advancing across the front lines. It has no challenge and no sex appeal.

But it works. People who back themselves up with lots of research always cross the finish line laps ahead of those who were too busy answering ads to take the time. In the job search, as in almost every other area of endeavor, nothing pays off like preparation.

We invite you to look upon the research assignments in this book, not simply as homework which has to be done, but as steps in a treasure hunt, tasks which will bring you closer to the hidden job gold *you* want. No one will grade your work, no one will scold you if you don't do it. And we want you to know that *we* know how strong the temptation is to skip ahead. If you are willing to go through the research stages now, and build the kind of opportunity base we recommend, we want you to know that from the depths of this book we applaud you.

Now back to work.

DIRECTORIES

The easiest work-related research source to tap into is usually a directory. There are, as we indicated above, thousands of directories which can give you an organized listing of almost anything. Once you have located the most appropriate directory, discover how the information is organized, and pick off the names and addresses of potential employers. If you have established an intelligent and willing information source in your job target field, ask him or her for the names of some of the most used directories in the field. But don't stop there; probe further. You will undoubtedly find out about some publications that even your contact isn't aware of.

The three most used business directories are *Standard & Poor's Register of Corporations, Directories & Executives; Dun & Bradstreet Million Dollar Directory* (or *Dun & Bradstreet Middle Market Directory*); and *Thomas' Register*—but don't let your imagination stop there.

YELLOW PAGES

The classified telephone directory is an amazingly valuable research tool. Using it, and your telephone, you can find out an amazing number of things about your job target areas. Not only will this free gold mine of information tell you what's happening in your city, but you can call the telephone company business office and request a free copy of the classified directory from any other city in the country.

INSIDE THE HIDDEN JOB MARKET

Let's follow the pattern of Sally Archer as she embarks on an abbreviated telephonic research campaign in her new job target, which is to be an artist's representative or a talent agent.

First move: Sally discovers that her telephone directory has no listings for talent agents and momentarily considers giving the whole project up.

Second move: After flipping pages for several minutes, Sally discovers three categories which seem to fit: *Theatrical Agencies, Artists' Agents,* and *Theatrical Managers and Producers.* "Not bad for a beginner," she thinks.

Third move: Time for the first phone call. Sally gets up, walks to the kitchen, avoids getting a Coke from the refrigerator, goes back to her desk, starts to doodle on the page. She selects a theatrical agency from the middle of the list: International Attractions, sounds good. She dials and then, as the phone starts to ring, quickly hangs up. "Damn. I don't know what I want to say," she mutters to herself.

Fourth move: Sally writes down three things she wants to find out on her first call: (1) Is there a trade association which she should know about? (2) What publications would be most logical for her to read? (3) What are the qualifications that are looked for in a talent agent? That's clear. "OK, let's go." Dial. Ring, ring. What's that? A recording! The number has been discontinued! Some nerve they have.

Fifth move: Same questions, another agency:

SALLY: Hello, may I speak to one of the agents, please?
VOICE: What's it in reference to?
SALLY: Um—well, I just wanted to get some information.
VOICE: Yes, well perhaps I can help you.
SALLY: Well, I don't know, I wanted to find out about your professional association.
VOICE: Our *what?*
SALLY: Oh, never mind. (Hangs up.)

Sixth move: Many more thoughts about this calling project: "Why go through this hassle? People aren't going to give out information. They don't know or care about me. On the other hand, what can I lose? I want to get this information, and I really can take a few more nos. It can't hurt."

Seventh move:

SALLY: Hi, this is Sally Archer, may I speak to one
 of your agents, please? Someone who specializes
 in dinner theater engagements.
VOICE: That would be Mr. Este. Can I tell him what
 it's in reference to?
SALLY: Sure, tell him that I'm writing an article
 about dinner theaters in this area, and thought
 that he could give me some information.
VOICE: Of course, just a minute please.
SECOND VOICE: John Este here.
SALLY: Hi, Mr. Este, this is Sally Archer. I understand
 that you specialize in dinner theater casts, and
 this is a field in which I'm doing some personal
 research, and I wonder if you have a minute.
SECOND VOICE: Sure, what do you want to know.
SALLY: Well, frankly, I'm most interested in the
 process you go through to line up your people,
 not just the actors, but, for example, the people
 in your agency. How does someone get into your
 business? It must be very difficult to break in.
SECOND VOICE: This business? First of all you
 have to be crazy, and then ...
 (fade out)

EPILOGUE

Sally got the information she wanted. She wasn't too encouraged at first, but after she made three or four other connections, she started to see that it wasn't at all hopeless. She learned about the publications, *Billboard* and *Variety*, and the two main unions: SAG and AFTRA. She met three or four people along the way, and talked herself into a good beginning job with an agency that specializes in casting commercials for ad agencies. Even now, she is starting to move up the ladder toward her target.

THIRD PARTIES

Many people keep it a secret when they are in the job market. They feel bashful about being reduced to looking for a job, so they don't want anyone to know. As a result they lose out on one of the most powerful job search tools: other people.

There is little doubt that the majority of your most productive job target leads will come out of your communications with others. Not only should you not hide your job search, you should specifically seek to bring others into the experience with you, and ask for their strong assistance and support.

A "third party" is any person, other than yourself and your ultimate employer, who can aid you in any way to find out about and locate your job targets. Third parties include your close circle of family and friends, a second-level cadre of people with whom you have a professional relationship, and an outer circle of people, whom perhaps you don't even know yet, who can help you put together powerful connections. Let's look at each of the three levels.

LEVEL 1: YOUR SUPPORT SYSTEM

Blood is thicker than unemployment. Your husband, wife, mother, father, children, uncles, aunts, and cousins all pulling together in the same direction could probably get you elected to public office if you really wanted it. They are eager to see you get what you want. Besides, they are probably tired of hearing you complain about the upcoming job search, and are more than ready to assist you. Here are some of the things which your family can provide. (If you're really ahead of your time, you'll let them read this section.)

Organizational support: To assist you in setting up a specific day-by-day, week-by-week job campaign plan, and then help you to follow it (a few nudges in the ribs).

Moral support: To remind you that who you are has nothing to do with your job title, or even whether you are working or not. To help unplug you from the automatic culture shock which accompanies unemployment or career change.

Financial support: Don't be afraid to ask, as far in advance as possible, for the specific financial support which you will need to carry you completely through your job campaign. Don't make the common mistake of pretending that you have more than enough money when you don't.

If you don't plan, the financial pressures will grow to the point where they preoccupy you, and result in a need for last-minute emergency aid which will put everyone on the spot.

TACTIC #32

Figure out a suitable weekly budget (not necessarily an austere one) and calculate how long it will realistically take for you to locate a new position that will nurture you. Add up your liquid assets, subtract your current liabilities, and divide the remainder by the weekly budget. Then compare the number of weeks you are financially prepared for with the number of weeks you estimate your directed job search will take.

If you have a shortfall, rather than try to squeeze your job campaign (it usually won't work), find a group of relatives who can each put up a small amount each month, spreading the load. Let them see how you have prepared your budget; it will give them confidence in your intentions.

Please don't make the mistake of "sparing" everyone your financial problem, and rushing into a crummy job to get the payroll started again. Don't sacrifice long-term satisfaction and fulfillment for short-term financial gain. You and your family will end up suffering for it.

COMPLETION CHECK [ ]

Personal feedback: Your family support system is probably close enough to you that you can get them to keep you in touch with what and how you are presenting yourself to the outside world. This means telling the truth to you about you, even when it is not what you want to hear. To accomplish this is a major achievement which will pay dividends for you and your family for years. Let your family know that you are willing to know, indeed, insist upon knowing, how you can improve your self-presentation. *It is crucial to this level of communication that you do not defend or explain yourself, even when you don't agree with the critique. Just "get" the communication.* Sample:

> YOU: How do you think I am coming across to employers, how can I improve my presentation?
> WIFE: Your suit always looks a little mussed when you go out.
> YOU: Thank you, I got it. What else?
> WIFE: I think you could use a new haircut.
> YOU: Thanks for telling me. How about the rest of me? Is there anything else?
> WIFE: I have never liked those shoes. I think they look old-fashioned.
> YOU: Thank you, I got it. What else?
> WIFE: I can't think of anything.
> YOU: Take another look, how can I improve my appearance or presentation?
> WIFE: Well, I really think the whole suit should go. It's four years old, and as I remember it was a cheap one to begin with. You don't look successful in it.
> YOU: Great, you're probably right. Thank you.

And so forth. You must know that all of us have set up such a defense system that it is virtually impossible for our friends to critique us at all. Many of them have tried, and been stopped short by our explanations and justifications.

The truth is powerful. Once you get the truth machine going in your family, you can feed it questions about your résumé, your verbal and nonverbal communications, your assertiveness, your budget, and your overall purpose.

TACTIC #33

Identify one or two people in your life whom you feel would be able and willing to critique your personal, job-directed presentation, and from whom you would be willing to accept and encourage feedback. When you have written their names down, write down five or six questions to ask, such as: How do you feel I can improve my job campaign? What could I do to improve my résumé? How would you suggest that I improve my personal appearance to look more successful? Where do you feel I am selling myself short? What do you feel my strongest job-related strength is? What is my weakest point? How can I improve my communication?

After you have organized the information you want to know, contact the people and tell them what you would like to do. Ask if they would be willing to give you an objective critique even if it involves some negative information. If you sense that they won't do it, thank them and find someone else.

COMPLETION CHECK ☐

Logistical support: A spouse or parent can help a lot in library research, preparing card files of contacts, canvassing organizations in advance, typing letters, keeping records, scheduling your travel, and keeping you to a time/money budget. Family members can make survey phone calls, take part in role plays, and critique accordingly.

An organized work area, with a family assistant, is an inspiration to you to keep the job information flowing clearly.

Scheduling: A family member who lives with you can be of valuable assistance in helping you keep to your self-imposed schedules and goals. This is best done by positive acknowledgment when the schedule is kept, and a specific critique when targets are missed. The schedule in question should be your *own* schedule that you agree to in advance. Your supporters don't need to berate you if you go astray, they can simply remind you to keep your own agreements.

Role playing: More hard work. But you don't have to worry much about it now. Later in the book we are going to set up a game for you to play which will give you direct feedback on how you present yourself in interviews. To do these role-play interviews you should enlist the aid of at least two others, one to play the role of employer representative, the other as observer and critic. Start now to think of who these two will be.

LEVEL 2: THE PROFESSIONAL CADRE

Within your circle of relationships you will undoubtedly find a number of professionally established men and women who can add depth and scope to your job market research. Some may be personal or family friends and contacts; others may be people you get in touch with from time to time on your own.

In talking about "professionals," we are rather imprecisely including all persons engaged in work which normally carries with it a certain social standing and credibility, and also involves a reasonable amount of public contact: lawyers, bankers, accountants, doctors, clergymen, consultants, therapists/counselors, executives or managers, professors, authors of books or articles in your chosen field.

People in these fields traditionally have access to many contacts in business, education, political, and social circles. They can generally open doors, get meetings arranged and questions answered. Their recommendations generally carry the weight of position behind them, and they can open up avenues which would take you longer on your own.

Warning: Treat your professional contacts as though they were face cards in a poker hand. Don't waste the contact with sloppy communication or lack of your own participation. Resist the temptation to turn them into substitute parents, or to lean on them too heavily with your problems, unless that is already the nature of the relationship.

Do your homework first, have a specific thing in mind, get to the point, and don't waste time. And when they have assisted you, acknowledge and thank them for the information, contacts, and the contribution they have made.

Here are some of the kinds of assistance you can get from the professionals in your life:

- Introductions to executives in firms related to your needs
- Knowledge of organizational changes which are not yet public knowledge
- Information interviews with authorities in your fields of interest
- Names of organizations which have developed and are trying to cope with particular problems
- Knowledge of openings which are about to be announced
- Suggestions about career choices
- Referral to specific information sources
- Résumé review or critique
- Recommendations and referrals to particular employers

TACTIC #34

Write down the names of everyone you know and anyone you know of who you would consider to have professional standing, or to be good contacts, whether or not you think they would help you. List as many as you can. Then go back over your list, and underline those you would be willing to contact.

Get their phone numbers, and start to contact them.

COMPLETION CHECK ☐

By staying in touch with the professionals in and around your life, and by letting them know what you are looking for and what you need to know to put your job campaign together in a straightforward and organized way, you will almost invariably increase the

INSIDE THE HIDDEN JOB MARKET   137

range of your work search campaign. Of course, you will still get your share of NO NO NO between the yeses, just as we promised you would, but stay with it; if the person doesn't have the information you seek, see if she/he can recommend someone else. Ask if you may follow up later. Acknowledge the person for her/his time and assistance. If warranted, send a nice thank-you letter.

LEVEL 3: OUTER CIRCLE

There's more. As you are beginning to see, there is a universe of available outside support through which you can expand your knowledge of and contact with the vast hidden job market. A third group of people who can serve as information sources are persons with whom you do not have a personal link, but who by the nature of their business are in daily touch with changes in direction and opportunity in a given field or industry, or even in a variety of industries.

This group includes, but is not limited to:

Salespersons
Personnel managers
People experienced in the field
Editors, and publishers of trade publications
Brokers (real estate, financial, insurance)
Employment service employees
Career counselors
College placement officials

It also includes private employment agents, career counseling firms, and executive recruiters.

Picture yourself in the center of a vast information retrieval system which includes virtually everyone at any level who has a connection to your job target field. Literally anyone you can reach by phone or mail or in person is a potential source of information from which to develop the names of employer prospects.

Contacting these information sources will take a little doing on your part. Who are they? Why would they talk to me anyway? Look at this as an exciting opportunity to expand your range on the phone. For example, you know that the Aztec Electronics Company in Phoenix, Arizona, is doing the exact kind of work in hi-fi components that you have lined up in your own job target. Fearlessly you call the sales manager long distance, person to person. You get his name and the call is put through on the first attempt. You introduce yourself as one who is trying to learn more about the field, conducting some research or finding out who's who in the industry. You use the three questions you have prepared in advance and get the information smoothly. The key to tapping these outer circle third-party sources is your willingness to give up your ideas about why it might not work, such as the fear that you might get rejected (you will, sometimes), and the variety of other excuses which will occur to you to convince you of the futility of the task.

The job market information you require is out there waiting for you now. The sources are at hand, the third parties are at their desks waiting for the phones to ring, the operators are standing by. All is in readiness. Are you willing to do it? (Answer yes or no.)

TACTIC #35

Through some telephone or library research obtain the names of ten people you didn't know before, who can possibly help you in your job search. You can get these potential contacts by calling organizations, asking your friends, or lifting names from articles, brochures, or letterheads.

COMPLETION CHECK ☐

You have acquired a set of keys for unlocking the hidden job market. No small accomplishment, as you will find out. By selecting and using these information sources you will have initiated a process which will result in your discovering and creating rewarding work opportunities which are not public knowledge. With this knowledge and the experiences it will produce in practice, you can shape your future time after time. What you've just learned is the first step. The next step follows:

PULLING IT TOGETHER

From all the sources we have described, you will now start to obtain the names and addresses of employer prospects in your job target fields. At this point you are simply collecting names and addresses. Except for the occasional happenstance, you have no idea whether these employers have jobs available in your target or not. Soon you will know, but now you are at the broad end of the research funnel. The idea is to build up a quantity of raw material for the refining process which follows.

Make an organized campaign out of this job market research, or you can get swamped in confusion.

- Decide on the half-dozen or so prime sources from the selection you have gathered, and plan to work on three or four at a time.
- Purchase the directory or publication, or use them at the library.
- From your research sources, start a file of 3 x 5 index cards with the names, addresses, and phone numbers of the employers and organizations you plan to contact.
- Be as specific as you can about each source selected. For example, from a directory of businesses in a particular field, extract only those names located in the geographic areas which interest you, or select only organizations of a given size.
- On each employer card, make a note of the source so that you can find out which sources work best for you.
- Create a *minimum* of 50 cards, 50 potential employers, for each of your job targets before you start the actual calling.
- When you discover that a particular source is not producing the names you are looking for, switch to a more productive one or change from one job target to another.

TACTIC #36

Set aside 10 to 15 hours, in one or two sessions, for the sole purpose of contacting or using the various sources you have come up with, to uncover the employer prospect names you seek. Keep going until you have listed at least 50 names in one of your job targets. Enter the name of each employer target on a separate 3 x 5 card.

COMPLETION CHECK [ ]

When you have 50 employers' names and addresses and phone numbers for each of your job targets, *stop*.

YOU DID IT. Congratulate yourself. Treat yourself to a day off—go to a musical, bring home a bottle of champagne, take a bubble bath, get high, go to the beach. But only when you've gotten the job done. If you're still getting around to doing your research, sorry, you'll have to save the celebration for later. Right now, it's back to the drawing board.

THE HIRING AUTHORITY

Q. Who do I want to contact in my job search?
A. The person who can make the decision to hire you.
Q. Who do I want to send my résumé and cover letter to?
A. The person who can make the decision to hire you.
Q. Who do I want to talk to on the phone about how I might fit into the organization?
A. The person who can make the decision to hire you.
Q. Who is the person who can make the decision to hire me?
A. The person who can make the decision to hire you.
Q. Is it personnel?
A. Sometimes, not usually.
Q. Is it the company president?

INSIDE THE HIDDEN JOB MARKET   141

A. Sometimes, not usually.
Q. How do I find out who it is?
A. Good question. We'll try to help you answer it.

In most organizations, with the exception of government or highly bureaucratic firms, the hiring decision is made by the line supervisor with whom you will work with on a day-to-day basis plus, generally, a recommendation from personnel and the approval of his/her boss.

In most organizations, if you have the solid backing of the line supervisory or department head you will get the offer unless someone turns up some skeletons in your broom closet.

This means that the person you want to identify within an organization is the manager or supervisor in charge of the function you wish to perform. In a small organization it may be a department manager or even a vice-president. In a larger firm the supervisor will be further down the line, depending upon your own reporting/salary level. We can't give you a hard and fast rule to follow; you will have to find out on your own who the hiring authority is for you.

How to find out: If you are familiar with the working situation in your job target field, you probably have an idea of the title you seek. If not, call the company switchboard and do what you need to do to get it:

> YOU: Hi, this is Ken Derry. I need to know the name of your, uh, I think the title is installation engineer.
> SWITCHBOARD: What?
> YOU: What is the name of the person who is in charge of the engineering for all your new ventilating installations?
> SWITCHBOARD: I'm sure I don't know.
> YOU: Do you have an engineering department?
> SWITCHBOARD: Just a minute, I'll connect you.
> YOU (under your breath): Damn . . .
> VOICE: Engineering.
> YOU: Oh hi there, this is Ken Derry. Could you give me the name of the person who is in charge of the engineering on all new installations?

VOICE: Would you want military or commercial installations?
YOU: Uh, let's see—commercial.
VOICE: Yes. Well that would be Mr. Sadek.
YOU: Could you spell that?
VOICE: S—A—D—E—K. Mr. Dwight Sadek.
YOU: Oh, thank you. By the way, could you give me his exact title?
VOICE: Let's see—it's contract manager.
YOU: Thank you very much, and while I've got you on the line, do you know if he reports directly to the marketing manager?
VOICE: I think so. That would be Mr. Alvo: A—L—V—O.
YOU: Great. Thank you.
VOICE: You're welcome.

If you have any difficulty at the switchboard level, have the call transferred to the department itself, or even to the president's office, where you are sure to find someone who knows who is in charge of what.

TACTIC #37

> Allocate at least one day's phone calling for you, or someone in your support system, to obtain the names of the specific hiring authority at each of the employer prospects you have written on your 3 x 5 cards. Make the calls matter of fact and professional. Don't talk with the party yet; just get the names. If someone asks why you want to know, say you have some material to send, and want to make sure it gets to the right person.
>
> COMPLETION CHECK ☐

AN URGENT MESSAGE FROM PERSONNEL

"Your tactics appear to leave us out of the hiring process, where we actually play a very valuable part.

Please explain or correct the misconception immediately."

Yes. We will.

Personnel is a very valuable, almost indispensible, part of the normal employment process in virtually all major organizations. In recent years its importance, and the value of its contribution, has expanded considerably in light of more sophisticated hiring parameters and human resource development goals within organizations. We absolutely support personnel and the services which they provide.

"But wait a minute," personnel says, "just one minute ago you told us . . ."

Yes. Here's the distinction. In the recruitment and hiring role, a large majority of personnel departments are concerned primarily with filling known or recognized positions which have been forwarded to them by departments with clear needs.

In the system which we are presenting here, where you are not chasing after advertised positions, but rather looking for ways to uncover opportunities which haven't yet been announced, or in many cases even noticed, you are more likely to uncover these situations at the line level rather than in personnel.

You *will* have to meet with someone from personnel at some point in your job search. You might find that this will be required even before you meet with the person whose interest you have stimulated on the phone, or most likely, after a successful meeting you will be scheduled to meet with personnel.

In some cases, when you are calling in to find out about needs to be filled or unadvertised positions, you might be requested by a secretary or assistant to call personnel. Try to keep from doing this if you can, and stay with your intention until you talk with the person who would make the hiring decision or would know about future situations.

Q. So who do I call?
A. The person who can make the hiring decision.

THE INFORMATION INTERVIEW

Brad Jennings

Brad Jennings went to MIT for his undergraduate work in engineering, and by the time he got his BS, he was clear that one of the last things he wanted to do with his life was to be an engineer. He shifted to Harvard where he picked up a Master's in English Literature, and then glided into a comfortable job as an English teacher at a fancy boys school in Connecticut. He even bought a pipe to go with his tweed jacket.

In two years Brad was dissatisfied with being a school teacher:

> There was far too much regimentation—I was pretty well stuck with the curriculum they gave me and I had to do it their way. I didn't see how I would last on the prospective salary curves and frankly, I needed more challenge.
>
> So in March, when contract time came around, I told the headmaster I wouldn't be renewing my contract for the Fall. I finished out the school year, and actually got paid through August, so I was able to take the summer off with ease. At our family place up in Small Point, Maine, I spent about four hours a day in an old rocking chair out on the front porch making lists of possible job targets. This was in '66 and guys my age were making killings in the money market and getting rich overnight. Of course, every so often a couple would get knocked out of the tree, and go squash, but I was always a crap-shooter at heart, so I kept coming back to the investment banking business as an exciting area to work in.
>
> But how? I had very little idea of what to do to get in and make my mark. I knew next to nothing about finance. Who would be crazy enough to hire an ex-engineer school teacher?
>
> However, I was relatively foolhardy at the time, and decided to go after it: a career in money! I knew that I would have to immerse myself in the subject so I could at least talk a good game. The first thing I thought of was that I should go back

to school and take some finance courses, perhaps get an M.B.A. 'The hell with it,' I finally said. And off I went to Manhattan, with little more to go on than a couple of books about making a killing in the stock market.

My strategy, which I picked up from a career counselor was not to look for a job at all. Really, instead of going out pounding the pavements looking for a job, what you do is to go out in search of *information* about jobs. It's like going on a big game hunt, and taking a camera rather than a rifle.

The technique, quite simply, was to locate people in the field who were successful and well thought of, to contact them personally by phone, and then to let them know how terrific you have heard they are, that you are very interested in what they are doing, and wish to discuss the financial field with them—man to man sort of.

I got a head start from our alumni association. I was able to get the names of at least a dozen of my old classmates who were now into finance. Not bad for a bunch of engineers—perhaps there was hope. A couple of them had the kind of names that you would associate with the landed gentry, or a prestigious law firm. I decided to save these for last.

It worked beautifully. After I had read three or four books, and a half dozen back copies of *Business Week* and *Fortune*, and subscribed to the *Wall Street Journal*, I was on my way. I started with the goal of meeting five new people a week, beginning with my ex-classmates. We would have lunch at the Harvard Club, talk about the good old days, and then retire to the lounge where I would pull out my notebook and start the interrogation from questions I had made up: What were the small companies on the make? What did they do? What kinds of people worked there? Who succeeded and why? What were the problems to be solved? I always ended up with two reasonably standard questions: First, what names could he give me of people who were successful in this game? My objective was to get a referral to two other people

for each person I met. This assured me of a constant
supply of meetings. I got so that I could actually
get names of people in a very particular area that
I wanted to explore: commodities, offshore
financing, acquisitions and mergers and so forth.
I felt like a reporter researching a story.

My final question was always to ask them to
explain some area which they had probably
assumed I knew already. My dumb question I called
it. It went something like this: 'Do you mind if I
ask a really dumb question? Could you explain to
me how commodity futures work?' Or whatever
I wanted to learn that week.

No one took offense, and most were happy to
give me a 15-minute course. I would supplement
whatever they told me by getting a book, or going
to the 42nd Street Library and looking up articles
on the subject. To make a long story short, I logged
something like 50 meetings in three months. The
cardinal rule was to never talk about looking for
a job. Never.

If they wanted to know why I was interested I
had no problem telling them the truth: I was
looking at a lot of different areas in banking and
finance, with a goal of selecting a particular area
in which to develop my skills. Never, 'I'm looking
for a job, can you help me?' After every meeting
I would send a thank you note and mention that I
hoped they wouldn't mind if I contacted them in
the future.

The job offers started to flow on their own.
People I had met would call me a few weeks later,
and say that a friend of theirs was looking for
someone to do something, and was I interested ...
I politely declined a number of these, because
towards the end of the campaign I had decided that
what I wanted was to work directly for one of the
top people in the field. To watch a genius at work,
to learn from a master.

And this is what happened: Brad Jennings rose
quickly in the field. He worked for three years with one
of the top "deal brokers," and gained a strong reputa-

tion for being able to evaluate new technologies and organizations. He became a partner in a small young investment banking firm, one of the few that survived the recession of the early 70's. Within five years of his entry into the field, his income was in excess of $100,000 per year. And, knowing Brad, it has probably moved up since then.

The information interview is one of the most powerful tools you can mobilize in your work search. This conclusion has been confirmed by most of the experts in the counselling field: Boles, Haldane, Jamison and Irish, and proven by example after example. There are dozens of ways to structure this approach for yourself, so long as you keep the cardinal rules in mind:

- Find out who the most successful people and organizations are in your job target field.
- Meet as many of them as you can.
- Always have particular questions prepared in advance.
- Never initiate discussions of your job search.
- If they start to talk about possible job openings appear interested, but not needy.
- In every meeting develop the names of at least two other people you can meet.
- Keep your energy and enthusiasm up. Stay on purpose.
- Send thank you notes after the meetings.

Once you have completed the information cycle, if you haven't uncovered a particular job possibility that interests you, you can recontact your list, letting each person know that you have decided to go for a particular job target where you feel you can make a contribution, and thank them for having helped you reach that point. Ask if they have any specific ideas of who might be able to use your abilities, or tell them how you feel you might be able to assist *them* in what they are doing. Keep it light but remain firmly in control. Communicate as equals.

TACTIC #38

Start your Information Interviews at the same time as, or before, your pitch for job interviews. Select five or six of your employer prospects; or others to whom you had a personal referral, and start scheduling meetings for the purpose of gathering information, expanding your contacts, and planting seeds for future harvesting.

COMPLETION CHECK

SAVOIR FAIRE

To successfully handle the information interviewing cycle you will need to reinforce your natural ability to be with successful people. Sometimes the tendency, particularly if there is some degree of panic in your job campaign, is to want to throw yourself at the feet of the nearest expert and ask for help. A very natural, common, and understandable tendency. And it doesn't work to act it out. It doesn't work at all.

We didn't say not to have your feelings. You will have these feelings (or not) regardless of what we say or do, or how much you wish you didn't. Go ahead and acknowledge them, and then set yourself up to demonstrate the real power you have underneath these interim job anxieties.

Here are some specific steps you can take to offset the normal pressures associated with the "failure syndrome" which frequently accompanies many people's work search:

- Make an anxiety list. List all the thoughts and feelings associated with yourself and your work search that come to mind, even if you aren't certain whether or or not they are true. Don't stop to analyze. List emotions, attitudes, self-images, fears of failure and rejection, and anything else. Outflow, as they say.
- Redo the above list frequently. Anytime you feel stopped or blocked, take a look at your experience of

yourself right then and list what you find. Don't repeat things which were on last week's list if they aren't true today.
- Communicate. Find someone in your support system to whom you can communicate your anxiety list, who will be willing to just "get it" and not reinforce it with extra sympathy or pity. Let him or her know your purpose is not to set him or her up as a parent figure, but simply to communicate. His or her only role is to receive your communication and acknowledge it.
- After you have written your list and communicated it, ask yourself this question: *Am I willing to allow all of these things to be true in my experience today, and to express myself powerfully anyway?* Don't lie. If the answer is no, then you need to go back and do some more communicating. You need to become the "observer" of your anxieties rather than the victim of them. Once you are able to observe and describe anxieties truthfully and accurately, then you won't have to act them out.
- Stay with the process until you feel released.
- Relax before going to the phone or on an interview. Consciously set yourself up for a ten-minute silent period in a comfortable chair with a minimum of outside distractions. Uncross your arms and legs and remain in the same position for the entire time. You may keep your eyes open or closed. Don't try to do anything in particular. Just observe your thoughts and your breathing. If you are into meditation, do that.
- Allow time before work-related meetings to think about your purpose. Write it down on a card and take it with you.
- Dress to win. Put yourself together in the best business or work-style clothes you have. Get someone to tell you accurately how you look. Clothes must be fresh and clean, and match the occasion.
- Monitor yourself in meetings. You don't want to talk too much. When you ask a question, stay alert for the answer. Watch your mind wandering and bring it back home. If you aren't clear about an answer you receive, admit it and ask the question again. Occa-

sionally pause (mentally) to observe yourself: How are you holding your body, where are the tensions? Lean back, let yourself go, and R E L A X.
- Acknowledge the other person in an interview or meeting. Compliment her or him if it's appropriate, let her or him experience your appreciation, but not your dependency.
- Consider yourself an equal (you are) in the relationship, and notice any tendencies to play yourself down. Watch out for bragging, which is generally a manifestation of insecurity.
- Refresh your vitality. Get sufficient rest, and don't think about or work on job search-related tasks more than five hours per day. Keep your mind engaged in other areas.
- Make a game out of it.

TACTIC #39

List at least five personal characteristics or attitudes which you feel could get in the way of a fully effective information interview campaign. Be very honest with yourself, and include things about your appearance, your attitude, your emotions or self-image, and any other personal factor which could inhibit you in this cycle.

COMPLETION CHECK

JOB CREATION

Jobs are a scarce natural resource to be allocated sparingly by the powers that be to a favored few and held back from the young, the old, women, Chicanos, and blacks. True or false?

False. This is what slots are about, not jobs. A slot is a budgeted opening for a job which has somehow lost its apparent value and become a number on someone's long list. It is work reduced to its most mundane and dehumanized level. Slots can be allocated and dis-

INSIDE THE HIDDEN JOB MARKET

tributed by government agencies and other bureaucracies, and parceled out politically or charitably. When the president asks Congress to create jobs he is actually talking about slots.

The people who work in slots hate the work and the people they work for. The people at the top don't have much respect for the people down in the slots either. Slots rob people of a working job.

This book is not about slots, it is about jobs.

A job is an opportunity to solve a problem, to create value for others, and satisfaction for yourself. A job involves a relationship with the world you live in. A job isn't the duties which describe it, it is the results which are produced.

Right now, and in the foreseeable future of the hemisphere, there is absolutely no limit to the jobs to be done, and those who would have you believe there is a limit, are either lying or don't understand the truth about jobs. By the way, most government agencies and many economists and educators don't know about jobs. They look at them upside down as something created by government or big business, rather than as a reflection of the productivity and value of a magnitude of individuals. But all you need to know now is that the number of jobs (not slots) available in today's workworld is unlimited.

Q. I don't get it.
A. Good. Is there a limit to the number of jobs available today?
Q. Yes, there is.
A. Great. Who sets the limit?
Q. I don't know, but it's obvious, otherwise more people would be working.
A. What are these people doing to locate jobs?
Q. I don't know, I guess many of them have given up, others are waiting for jobs to be advertised.
A. Yes, so there is a limit to the number of *advertised* jobs.
Q. Right.
A. Now do you see any areas of our economy right now that are experiencing problems?

Q. Are you kidding? It's all screwed up: pollution, transportation, energy, health, education. There aren't any good movies around. Even TV stinks.

A. Exactly. But doesn't mean that there are jobs?

Q. Not as far as I see.

A. Oh, no? Take any industry, think of any one.

Q. OK, I got one.

A. What is it?

Q. Health food. I got fired from a job in a health-food store. They said that there was a depression. Not enough people buying health food these days. At least around here. I tried several other stores—same story.

A. Good example. No jobs in health-food stores because of low sales. So what is a problem that they face?

Q. What do you mean?

A. What is a problem faced by the health-food stores in this area? You just said it.

Q. Oh, a problem they face is low sales.

A. Right. Did you look for a job in sales?

Q. No, I was in purchasing.

A. Do you have any ideas how the stores could increase their sales?

Q. Oh, yeah. There are a lot of things they could do, they don't do any promotion at all. They are very unimaginative in how they display and package their stuff, how they ...

A. Hold on, do you see that if you got very clear about how a particular store could increase its sales, you could get a job as a salesman or sales manager?

Q. You mean go in and tell them I'm a salesman.

A. Yes.

Q. I hadn't thought of that.

A. That's right. There are an unlimited number of jobs around if you are willing to see them as problem-solving opportunities.

Q. Even in big industries?

A. Particularly in big industries. These guys need all the help they can get. They may lay off ten thousand workers who all end up sitting around waiting for someone else to figure out what to do next.

INSIDE THE HIDDEN JOB MARKET 153

Q. Well, how come the people who don't have jobs aren't out looking for problems they could solve so they could get back to work?
A. Most of them don't know how. No one ever told them that they could.
Q. Really?
A. Really.

REMINDERS AND REFERENCES

Reminders

- Your future worklife is not in the "help wanted" columns. Believe it.
- Identify prospective employers not on the basis of ads, but by contacting enough people in firms to uncover opportunities which are not public knowledge.
- Every job search is a series of no's followed by yes. To get what you want, create more no's faster.

References

The Hidden Job Market by Tom Jackson and Davidyne Mayleas. Quadrangle, New York, 1976.

Special Recommendations for Women:

From Kitchen to Career: How Any Woman Can Skip Low-level Jobs and Start in the Middle or at the Top by Shirley Sloan Fader. Stein & Day, Briarcliff Manor, N.Y., 1977.

Getting Yours: How to Make the System Work for the Working Woman by Letty Cotton Pogrebin. Avon Books, New York, 1976.

Super Directories

Guide to American Directories. B. Klein & Company, 11 Third Street, Rye, New York 10050.

Encyclopedia of Associations. Gale Research, Book Tower, Detroit, Michigan 48226.

Business Publication Rates & Data. Standard Rate & Data Service, Inc., 5201 Old Orchard Road, Skokie, Illinois 60076.

Directories

Standard & Poors' Register of Corporations. Standard & Poors, 345 Hudson Street, New York, N.Y. 10014.

Dun & Bradstreet Million Dollar Directory and *Dun & Bradstreet Middle Market Directory.* Dun & Bradstreet, 99 Church Street, New York, N.Y. 10007.

Thomas' Register. Thomas Publishing Co., 461 Eighth Avenue, New York, N.Y. 10001.

Question: Are you willing to put in some work to get the job that works for you? The investment in job market research will pay back bountifully in increased job satisfaction and earnings.

7

THE UNIVERSAL HIRING RULE

THE AUTOMATIC WORK MACHINE

Most of us are schooled to believe that a job is a gift which is bestowed by society in honor of our having passed successfully through the rocks and shoals of the passage from childhood to adulthood. The job is our way of knowing we made it.

When no job is "awarded" we fall into the other side of the equation: feelings of remorse, self-doubt, apathy —common childhood attitudes—are easily observed in unemployed at all ages. The experience of being fired or terminated can turn grown men and women into babies.

Schools relentlessly drive home the message: "Dropouts don't get jobs," "If you don't study, you won't get a good job." Go to college, study hard, wash behind the ears, do your homework, marry the boss's daughter. A good job is the prize.

In counseling circles the underlying message is frequently the same: If you don't have a job you are in trouble. It's parent/child, doctor/patient all the way. Public service counselors whose own worklife is frequently entangled in red tape, zero feedback, and next to no acknowledgment, bestow job possibilities like charity. It is not surprising that in the view of a "disadvantaged" applicant, work ends up somewhere between remedial reading and reform school.

This is to let you know that the system is rigged. Work is not the prize. *It is the game itself.* And like any other game you play, you will experience a far greater degree of satisfaction and reward if you enjoy playing it than if you are only concerned with keeping score.

Our contemporary attitudes toward work spring in large part out of the industrial revolution, when a person's ability to be in a unique relationship with the

THE UNIVERSAL HIRING RULE 157

world and to produce value was subjugated into a system to support the machines. Anyone could tend to the steam engine or loom, or mine the coal, or lay the tracks, or carry the cement, or file the unending flow of paperwork. A job was a job was a job.

The educational system quickly fell into alignment with the needs of the factory system which grew out of the industrial revolution. Workers' kids were taught how to be workers. Bosses' kids were taught how to be bosses.

And you generally stayed put. Too many job changes were a sign of instability or a disagreeable temperament. And employers weren't looking for *that*. Whatever you did, in the industrial-based employment system, you didn't want to get fired. As little as a generation ago, being fired from a job could literally be the end of a career and of the opportunity to participate in life in any terms other than poverty and failure.

In short, the foundations of the employment/education structure which operates for most people today were laid down to support a factory job-oriented system at a time when the prime motivation was increased production and maximized profits, with little concern for the satisfaction of the workers.

Even shorter: Few people realize how completely the rules of the game have changed, and that it is now possible to identify and locate jobs which bring you personal satisfaction and reward and create strong value for the employer, plus a good paycheck for you.

EMPLOYMENT OF HUMAN RESOURCES

There is an enormous number of jobs to be done in the world today, a number continually expanding beyond the ability of people to even catalog, let alone fill. Please stop to think about that for a few minutes. Just close your eyes. Get a picture of a field of endeavor or industry, and think of as many things as you possibly can which aren't working right. Go ahead, spend one minute with your eyes closed. How many problems can you come up with? Then you can move on to:

TACTIC #40

Select one of your job targets. Under it, list every specific problem or task you can think of which would be involved in this job target. In other words, analyze the specific components of the job target in terms of the problems which are solved by it.

COMPLETION CHECK [ ]

It is important for you to become very, very clear about the problems which exist in the world around you, particularly in your own field of interest. It is your conscious awareness and your ability to spot these problems which enables you to navigate the employment market with facility. That's why we keep coming back to it.

It is obvious that the world is utilizing only a minuscule portion of its innately available human problem-solving resources. People are essentially immobilized when it comes to dealing with their world. At the human level people are hurt, confused, misunderstood. At the industrial level organizations don't quite know how to adapt their techniques to new demands or new constraints to provide value economically. At the world level we don't know how to feed, clothe, or house our population, or how to preserve our resources, or how to enhance people's sense of purpose and aliveness.

It is through the employment process that the world's human resources are deployed against the world's problems and needs. It is the failure of this process which allows the world to remain deep in problems and at the same time have countless millions of its people not working.

Q. May I ask a question?
A. Yes, what?
Q. Is this supposed to be a book about how I can get my worklife more together?
A. Yes.

Q. I thought so. Well, why the hell are we dealing with all this stuff about world problems, hunger, environment, and so forth? I read the paper. I know that things are all . . . screwed up. I really do, what I want to know about is what to do for me.

A. OK, I got it. You want to get practical.

Q. Yes, I'm getting sleepy with all this stuff.

A. OK, I'll move on, but we really need to make one more very important point first.

Q. All right, but please keep it short, then I want to know about this universal hiring rule you promised.

A. It's a deal.

ONE MORE IMPORTANT POINT

Individuals, schools, government agencies, counselors, and others need to help expand the ability that people have to deal with their personal career campaigns. The lack of education and understanding in this area, whether it be on the part of black youths or blue-chip executives, is appalling, and costly in terms of the unemployed resources as well as the human downtime, suffering and economic costs.

The demonstrated fact is that the more trained a person is in the "delivery system" the more able that person is to devote full time and effectiveness to personal job search needs, and the more likely to achieve a job which produces personal satisfaction and a contribution to the growth of the society.

THE UNIVERSAL HIRING RULE

Any employer will hire any applicant so long as he or she is convinced that it will bring more value than it costs.

It's as simple as that. Employers will hire people who they feel will produce value for them. Let it sink in for a minute. Now put it in terms that will make sense to you in light of the problems you have already identified in your job target area:

ABC Packing would hire me if they felt I could design an attractive box which would cut their shipping costs by 20%.

Perry Productions would give me an interview in a moment, and probably hire me, if I showed them how to get new business from the airlines.

Mr. Blax would definitely offer me the job if I could somehow show him how to have the typing pool function better. We could probably even save my salary by cutting back on the night shift.

TACTIC #41

> Think of a potential employer in your job target area (real or imagined). Think of three problems which he probably experiences. Then write down a solution which you could provide with your own skills for each problem.
>
> COMPLETION CHECK ☐

THE BUREAUCRATIC EXCEPTION

Let us quickly tell you that there are, unfortunately, a few exceptions to the universal hiring rule. Large governmental structures, and other organizations where hiring is controlled by civil service, or where the ultimate user of your service is not involved in the hiring process, can present virtually insurmountable obstacles to your communicating the value you offer. The rule works in these situations when and if you can reach up to a high enough level so that you are communicating to someone who has the authority to respond to the application and an appreciation of the value you offer. But in many bureaucratic agencies this can be a long hard fight.

IF IT'S SO SIMPLE . . .

Listen to what some top corporate recruiters say about the applicants they see:

THE UNIVERSAL HIRING RULE

I'll swear that this woman I interviewed didn't even have the first idea of what we *did*. She spent most of the time trying to find out about the benefits.

> Bruce Bradon, personnel interviewer
> *Southern Chicle Reporter*

Seventy-five percent of the college kids we interview never get around to letting us know what they can do for us. They do a good job telling about their future interests and goals, but they forget to relate it to us.

> Alvin Zerkain, purchasing manager
> Forest Management Corporation

People call me all the time on the phone. "Do you have any openings?" is about standard. If they don't at least have an *idea* of what they could do for us, I give them the brush-off.

> Helen Charles, owner
> Rite Style Boutique chain

Please tell people, particularly if they are just entering the job market for the first time, to read up a bit on what the employer does so they can at least show that they care a little.

> Peter Jones
> Annapolis Marine

I guess what happens is that people get all mixed up in their fears and needs. It doesn't help them much. The ones who get the best offers are those who put a little sell in their presentation.

> Anita Powers, interviewer
> Aspect Computer Systems

It is simple. But most job seekers haven't gotten the word that the way to excite interest in a potential employer is to communicate how you, the applicant, can assist the employer in achieving results: literally, to communicate how the employer will easily benefit from the association. It isn't even so important that you have uncovered the secret to an outstanding complex problem—just plain old garden variety problems will do, unless you are in the upper tax brackets. It is the fact that you are willing to deal from a position of support and contribution that makes the biggest impression. This is music to an employer's ears.

OLD FAVORITE PROBLEMS TO SOLVE

As we said, the value you communicate doesn't have to be highly technical, or represent an ingenious breakthrough of a complicated problem (although if you have it, flaunt it—without, of course, giving away your secrets). You may not even have to do any research, as there are a number of standard problems or needs which apply pretty much across the board:

Cut costs
Make it look better
Get it done more quickly
Improve appearance
Increase sales
Expand (virtually anything)
Make the boss look good
Provide more information
Improve the profit picture
Open more territories
Diversify the risks
Cut staff costs
Get government support
Turn around a bad situation
Preserve competitive advantage
Improve the packaging
Avoid potential problems
Organize it
Expedite the workflow
Get faster delivery
Use old things in a new way
Cut downtime
Provide a tax advantage
Meet deadlines easily
Reduce inventories

TACTIC #42

Back to you, and your problem-solving abilities. List three achievements or accomplishments which you have been responsible for in your life—each one at the top of a page. Under each achievement list all the problem-solving skills which contributed to it. Keep expanding the list of things which you can do to produce value for others.

COMPLETION CHECK ☐

UNIQUE SELLING PROPOSITION

There is one thing which you can do better than anything else you do, and probably better than a lot of other people. What is it?

TACTIC #43

Write a paragraph which describes your version of your own most unique ability, in terms which show how you are valuable to another person or firm. Keep rewriting until you are clear that it is your best, clearest self-presentation. Then find a member of your support system, and verbally (without reading) communicate it to this person.

COMPLETION CHECK ☐

You are, indeed, a unique combination of skills, interests, abilities, education, training, accomplishments, experiences, memories, dreams, and illusions. There has never been one just like you, and there never will be another. You have the ability to excel in one or more areas, perhaps in directions you are not even aware of.

Ginny Bowen

I never worked out the way dear old mum wanted me to, bless her soul. I got fired from six jobs in seven years, and it was only by the love of God that I held on to the last one. People always wanted me for office management-type things, and I was ready to give it the good Irish try. But I would generally come to the same point as I told you about in Mr. Richter's office. It would boil down to the same bloody scene: "Why didn't you do this? What happened to that? I thought that you said you would . . ." I can't stand that stuff. Let's face it: I have a black Irish temper from my mother's side. Better than my father's drinking I guess. But office work and me come together like snake oil and water.

As a proper lady worker I was fairly out in the middle of the lake with nowhere to go, as they say. And no oars in that boat either. I had a bad record and no prospects, and that was that.

And no use pretending that you don't know how the sun rose over fat Ginny finally. It was your own people who found out about the artificial flowers. Who would think that people would pay their good dollars for dear old mum's pretty silk flowers. Not me. I made those flowers for ten years, giving them away to me worthless lovable friends for free. Mum taught me these skills when I was 15, and in ten years I gave away some arrangements you wouldn't believe—for friends' weddings and all. Forty or fifty beautiful silk flowers in one arrangement—prettier than any you could find in a garden.

And your smart lady counselor and her brains, thank God someone has 'em, telling me to cash in on any hobby, not to go after office work. And now my little shop doing so well. Now I know what work is. You use the gifts you have, not the ones you wish you had.

What is that thing which you can say about yourself that no one else could say quite so clearly? You may not be in touch with it. It's probably covered over with some other skills which you think are more practical, or maybe you haven't seen this side of you fully expressed.

After ten years away from the conventional workplace, rearing their children, we often see women come back to work. Rarely has a group so masked their capabilities and power as these women have. Most of them make a point of saying right away that they really don't have any work skills, and that what little skills they used to have are incredibly rusty. It often takes a serious confrontation by a trained job counselor or work therapist to push them through the pretense of powerlessness to the still valid skills and abilities under the surface, which are available to be called into play as needed the moment the player is willing to get into the game. The same thing is very often true of new college graduates, who possibly hold the group record for low self-esteem. It is amazing that after 14 or 16 years of education they have almost no sense of personal worth, or how to communicate it.

It's important to get in touch with the aspects in you which can make a unique contribution to the workworld, and to develop ways to let people know about them.

TACTIC #44

Write your own obituary. From your alive and healthy vantage point right now, think of the things which you feel you would most like to be remembered for when you pass on to the next level. Write the obit in the past tense starting with the words "She (he) is most remembered for her work in . . ." and write at least half a page.

COMPLETION CHECK

THE UNIVERSAL HIRING RULE (APPLIED)

Here, in outline form, are the specific steps which will result in your obtaining relevant job offers.

1. Achieve clarity and certainty about your job targets.

2. Recognize existing and potential problems (opportunities for solution and benefit) within job target areas.

3. Clarify and acknowledge your specific ability to contribute to the solution of the recognized problem.

4. Identify, within the job target area, the appropriate "power source" most concerned with the recognized problem area.

5. Clearly communicate your relevant problem-solving abilities to this power source in a way that gets him or her in touch with the value which you offer.

These five steps describe the underlying foundation of this book and system and, for that matter, any system which will effectively enable you to come from who you are into the workworld in a way which produces satisfaction and aliveness for yourself, and value for others. Let us follow these five steps in more detail.

1. ACHIEVE CLARITY AND CERTAINTY ABOUT YOUR JOB TARGETS

By this time, assuming you have followed the tactics concurrently with the text (if you haven't done the tactics yet, stay with us here anyway), you will have looked within yourself and located elements of personal interest and satisfaction, and areas of problem-solving capability, which you have combined into four specific job targets which you are willing to pursue. It is important to make these targets real for yourself so that you can focus your energy behind them and produce direct movement.

Without a target you are willing to go after, you will be tempted to change your direction each time you run into an obstacle. And unless you confront obstacles with energy, born of certainty, you won't get through them.

2. RECOGNIZE EXISTING AND POTENTIAL PROBLEMS (OPPORTUNITIES FOR SOLUTION AND BENEFIT) WITHIN JOB TARGET AREAS

This area of problem identification has been discussed several times, and will undoubtedly show up

THE UNIVERSAL HIRING RULE 167

again before we are through. We want you to get it. If you can go beyond the mere words and into your personal experience of the proposition, you will vastly expand your ability to master the workworld, or in practical terms, *to make more money and have more fun.*

You will have to get away from your idea that problems are "heavy" and to be avoided. *All of human endeavor exists in the context of problems to be solved.* That's the name of the game. Without any problems to solve, there is no game.

Where we get stuck is in staying with the same old problems year after year. It's as though we were afraid to give them up and move on. Look around you and you'll see that in people's private lives, as well as at work, they are tenaciously hanging on to the same old patterns:

- After five years together Mary and John are still trying to work out an agreeable way to make household decisions.
- Brad and Henry still haven't resolved their boyhood struggle to beat one another in sports.
- Helen Sparkes is still trying to lose weight. She's on her tenth diet.
- George Siegel is handling the same accounts he had three years ago.
- Ozzie and Sue are still looking for work as a comedy team. They go out on four or five auditions a month, and haven't had a gig for six months.
- Fred G. has had each of his three manuscripts turned down by publishers. He is bitter, but determined that his fourth book will make it.
- Francine is locked into a bad marriage, has known for five years that it isn't working, won't give it up.
- Sara has been trying for a year to prove to her boss that she can handle more responsibility. It is clear that he doesn't believe that a woman can do the job. She is determined to change his mind, if it takes years.
- Clarence has a small business which has been on the verge of collapse for two years. He is afraid to give it up. His personal identity is tied up in it totally.

When you solve a problem, wrap it up, and put it away you have completed your involvement with it, and are in a space to move on to another more challenging game.

You can also complete a problem by wrapping it up unsolved and handing it on to someone who can solve it. This is a valid way to handle problems, and often enables you to move quickly to higher levels of management.

It is also valid to abandon problems when you are stuck too long in them, or have reached the point where the potential payoff is no longer worth the effort. But in order to experience a sense of completion with a problem which you are abandoning, you must communicate clearly to yourself and others involved in it with you that you are abandoning it. If you do this clearly, rather than, as most of us do, sweep it under the rug, you will open up room to take on new problems and challenges and to expand.

Of the three techniques described for handling problems (solution, delegation, and abandonment) there is only one that will get you a position in the workworld, and that is *solution:* the entry point into all problem areas.

How to solve problems: The trick to problem solving (which most people miss) is to first *clearly identify the problem*—to be sure of what needs attention and possible correction; to identify the part of the transaction or process where the purpose or goal is being thwarted.

For example: A car is inoperative alongside a road. A person inexperienced with autos could describe the problem with: "The car won't go," and call a tow truck to haul it away. A more experienced person would first check the fuel, try to start the car, and come to the conclusion that the engine is inoperative. An even more experienced person would be able to check the fuel, battery, spark plugs, and starter, discover that the carburetor is flooded, and allow some of the excess fuel to drain off before starting the car and driving away.

Similarly in business: If sales and profit are off, the

THE UNIVERSAL HIRING RULE 169

sales manager will suggest that sales budgets be improved. The public relations department will be certain that more media exposure is needed. The new-product people will want to redesign the product. And the financial people will want to cut production costs.

As a problem solver, your task is to identify what the problem is, systematically disregard the parts or elements of the situation which are working properly, and then objectively look at the parts that aren't.

Probably 75% of the movement toward solution is identification and narrowing down. Once the key misalignment, or break in communication, or unconsciousness is clearly seen, the solution is often rather easy to uncover or design.

A problem is not necessarily something which is going wrong. It is any need or objective which is not yet achieved. Something becomes a problem when there is a clear description of a desired condition, and a recognition that the condition does not exist. The size of the problem is measured in terms of the "difference" or "potential" between the desired state and the way it is now.

You don't have to know about the particular problems of a specific employer to be able to communicate to that employer, although it helps. You can, if you know what is going on in the industry in general, or with another employer, interpolate to the needs of the particular employer in question.

Call people who are knowledgeable about the job target field. Find out from them what is going on, what people are talking about, what new directions or complications or shifts are occurring. Talk with trade association executives, editors of publications, experts, teachers, has-beens, comers. Listen and take notes.

The key to getting good information is being able to get on the phone expertly and often. Yes, it will frequently take several calls to get the information you want. It may take more calls than you expected. Keep pushing through your resistance to making the calls. Remember how the job campaign looks. It's NO NO NO NO NO NO, ditto 20 times, and then a big hit:

you will develop a contact which will get you in communication with the right people. This one source can make the entire game worthwhile.

The skills you are developing in this process are life skills which will pay dividends for years through an increased ability to control your life, and to continue to make a valuable contribution, as you keep in touch with the flow of life/world problems.

TACTIC #45

Gather the name and location of at least ten experts in one or more of your job target fields, by getting on the phone to one (from a referral or article), asking that person for the names of others with expertise in the field, and so forth. Don't stop until you have the name and phone number of at least ten experts. These names will be a strong backup resource for you to find out virtually anything you need to know in your field.

COMPLETION CHECK ☐

3. CLARIFY AND ACKNOWLEDGE YOUR SPECIFIC ABILITY TO CONTRIBUTE TO THE SOLUTION OF THE RECOGNIZED PROBLEM

We didn't say *solve* it, we said *contribute to the solution*. You don't need all the answers before you get on the job. The mere fact that you are willing to demonstrate an interest and ability in the area will put you ahead of most others, whose primary communication to employers is one of need and dependency. What works is for the potential employer to realize that your purpose in the relationship is to assist him in reaching *his* objectives.

To accomplish this, you need to get clear about your own capabilities and skills, and to be willing to frame them in words and phrases which you will be able to communicate.

Barrier: *People generally don't know what they can*

do. They are not in touch with their abilities. "It's not polite to boast," our mothers said. "Won't you ever learn?" said father. "How many times do I have to tell you?" the teachers repeat. "You're stupid!" we are told.

We are in a culture which doesn't know how to acknowledge the small everyday accomplishments and achievements. As a result, many of us have lost sight of them in ourselves. This is particularly true of people who are just entering or reentering the job market. Self-esteem is in the pits.

The average college student, the housewife returning to the workworld, can scarcely find a good thing to say about themselves. They've got it set in their minds that somehow the people "out there" with the good salaries, the attractive secretaries, private offices, and long expense account lunches, have all the answers. They know!

Secret: They don't know. It would shock and alarm you to find out how much pretense is in front of how much ignorance in the workworld. People who look like they know what's going on, don't necessarily. It is more and more frequently proved that experience is not a necessary measure of potential work success. Many people are stuck at a level of competence in which their jobs become replays of the same record. Their job is to find answers, to put out fires, to end failure, and they need all the help they can find.

You are able. Yes. You are able and competent and skilled and proficient, and probably perfect the way you are. Of course, you don't want to see it that way. You probably think that you will be just right—or perfect— only after you have completed five more courses, or gotten a promotion, or practiced your shorthand, or finished a training program. Or when you've managed to find the right mate, or saved enough money, or found the right job. No. That's not it. If you keep looking at all of the next things which you need to do to be able to be perfect, to be ready, you won't ever make it. The list is too long. Your demands are too high. *You are, right now, in your prime.* You will never be more ready than right now to move on. You are reading this book at exactly the right time. The perfect moment.

Q. You're crazy.
A. OK. Why do you say that?
Q. You're just crazy. I am not perfect, and I doubt that I ever will be, and I don't care if I am or not. Why waste valuable space with all of this Zen or est stuff now? I'm interested in something more practical.
A. Like what?
Q. Like getting a better job.
A. Any job?
Q. No. I did my homework. I know what my targets are. You made sense in that part.
A. Thanks. You have your job targets. That's good. Have you identified potential employers?
Q. Sort of. I've started the research, and I'm making progress. It's pretty boring though, as you said it would be.
A. Yes. Let me ask you something—what do you have to offer an employer?
Q. I think I'm very competent. I communicate well. I don't mind hard work. But I know that there is a lot to learn. I don't think I'm perfect. I don't think this is my prime. Not yet, I've got a lot of good years left.
A. I agree. As I see it, you are at a place where you have developed your skills and abilities to a point, and are getting clear about what you want to do, and what it will take to do it. Right?
Q. Right.
A. Well, that's what perfect looks like for you right now: being willing to be exactly where you are when you are there.
Q. I still don't get it. I haven't arrived, I'm still in the middle of it.
A. What you don't get is that when you are in the middle of something, the perfect place to be is in the middle of it.

What you will present to potential employers in your job target field is *the strongest possible description of your skills and abilities, described in terms which relate to solving problems the employer experiences.*

THE UNIVERSAL HIRING RULE

Incorrect: "I'm looking for a job. Do you have anything?"
Correct: "I'd like to show you some designs which you could sell very profitably."

Incorrect: "I've always been interested in publishing."
Correct: "My layout experience would help you in your new cookbook series."

Incorrect: "I'm an excellent typist."
Correct: "I could expedite your correspondence."

Probing for relevant skills: One of the things you will learn in your working experience, if you haven't already done so, is that even the most complex positions can normally be broken down into relatively simple, easy-to-understand components. Of course, the manager or executive holding down a $30,000-per-year position will probably be the last person to admit this. He or she has built up an immense wall of jargon and complications to render the position virtually indecipherable to outsiders. Beneath the facade lie the basic elements of most work transactions:

Planning
Feedback
Correction
Verbal and written communication
Interpersonal relations
Research and analysis
Measuring results
Selling or presenting
Delegating
Organizing

On top of the basics we have just described are, of course, specific technical skills and information. But, in most jobs, the actual use of these technical skills accounts for only 20 to 25% of the work done, and (be prepared to get a lot of argument here) much of that has been so specifically organized, so fragmented, that new people can pick up the techniques in a very short time.

A well-paid, experienced office manager confesses that she could teach someone virtually everything they would need to know to do her job in six weeks.

Paramedical and paralegal workers are handling tasks previously done only by doctors and lawyers.

Technicians are frequently able to handle engineering assignments within particular areas where there has been good on-job exposure.

People who have not been trained in management techniques frequently turn out to be well qualified to supervise others and produce results.

Keep probing for basic abilities. These are the building blocks with which even the most elaborate job structures are erected.

Once you have clearly identified or inventoried the basic skills, and are aware of the particular problem areas you wish to address, your task is to clearly express the skills in a way which directs them toward solving the problem.

TACTIC #46

List three job titles within your future objectives which you don't feel qualified to handle now. Then start to analyze the work done in these positions into categories of specific technical expertise and basic work skills. Separate what you feel you could learn rather easily from what will require technical knowledge.

COMPLETION CHECK ☐

4. IDENTIFY, WITHIN THE JOB TARGET AREA, THE APPROPRIATE "POWER SOURCE" MOST CONCERNED WITH THE RECOGNIZED PROBLEM AREA

For each problem area within your job target there is at least one person who cares; one person who would be willing to go out of the way to solve that problem. You may have to track through miles of organizational

THE UNIVERSAL HIRING RULE

spaghetti before you reach the place where someone acknowledges responsibility, coupled with an interest in getting to a solution. But there is such a person. It will be someone whose own career is tied up with the problem, but it is not always the most obvious person. We have seen people who you would think would have a strong interest in cleaning up a problem, perpetuate it—perhaps to sabotage their boss, or to hold on to their jobs. The game of "I told you so" is a favorite pastime in the working world as well as at the family or social level.

But there will be someone on the line who will be getting burned from the friction generated by the work problem(s) you uncover in your research. Someone is in the hot seat. To be of value to you, this person will have to be a "source of power" within the organization.

Translation: A source of power is a person with the ability to hire, to produce results, to allocate funds, and to determine other actions within the organization.

Example: Roberta Rich knew that she was potentially a very successful saleswoman, even though she hadn't done any "real" selling for the past eight years, while she was rearing her son Bert. She knew her sales skills were, if anything, better than when she had quit work, and she had demonstrated this in several nonpaying volunteer positions with various charities in the Dallas area, where she lived.

Instead of jumping into something easy and available at the time of her reentry, such as the real estate or beauty aids sales jobs which were frequently advertised, Roberta decided she would go further and see if she could get involved in something more oriented toward the booming business growth in the area.

For six weeks she read everything she could about business growth in the Dallas metroplex. She met people at the Chamber of Commerce, went through back issues of the business section of the *Dallas News* and *Times Herald*, and spent several days in the library reading *Business Week* and the *Wall Street Journal*, looking for particular areas which she felt would relate to her target of being a salesperson to new businesses. Roberta put together a list of a dozen or so product areas, which she considered, including everything from computers to furniture to temporary help services.

When she boiled it down, the top item on her list of product areas to sell in was printing services, and the second item was business forms. "I don't know how it worked out like this," she said, "except that I became very aware that the one thing which every business had was paper. Tons and tons of printed forms, brochures, letterheads, manuals. You name it. So if business was booming, you could be certain that printing sales were booming too."

After she had familiarized herself with many of the basics of the trade, enough so she could handle the jargon, and had spent some time with a couple of printing salesmen she was able to meet through a business friend of hers, she decided to launch her own self sales campaign.

Roberta's initial approach, which was to get a list of printers from the Dallas and Forth Worth Yellow Pages and call and ask for the sales manager, didn't work. She rarely got through, her calls were not returned, and when she did get through she didn't make much headway.

Undaunted, she tried another tack: "I decided I wanted a bit more clout behind my opening strategy," she said. "I needed to have more time to demonstrate that an ex-housewife with no experience could compete in a predominantly male industry. I knew that I could sell, and I only needed 15 minutes face to face to prove it."

Roberta shifted her tactics masterfully. Instead of making cold calls to the printers, she picked the 50 largest business firms in the area and called the office managers or buyers who were responsible for buying printing. She got through to 25 or 30 of them, and explained her objectives: She saw herself as a terrific saleswoman, she was interested in breaking into a new field that was particularly difficult for a woman, and she needed their assistance. She got these large purchasers of printing to give her the names of the sales managers, or the owners, of the firms they did business with. In a few cases they made the phone call for her, but mostly she would make her own call, using the name of the corporate connection as a reference to successfully get her interviews.

In three weeks she had 12 interviews and 4 offers. The one she took allowed her to work pretty much on her own and to open up new accounts, which she did successfully. In two years she had built up such a following that she set up her own printing brokerage business.

Implied referral: Something to notice in this last example is the power of having a referral or "implied referral" from someone in the field. The working world is so inbred that it is often necessary to drop a few names to unlock doors that are instinctively closed to outsiders. But these names don't have to be people you know intimately or personally. It can be someone you have talked to briefly over the phone. Look for natural relationships—a supplier, a customer, a higher-level executive in the same firm, a noted authority, a friend, a school chum, a social connection—to reveal to you and introduce you to the power source you need to contact.

TACTIC #47

Accumulate some "power" in your job search. Start finding out the names of some of the people who can make a difference in your getting what you want: people at or close to the top in your particular job target. Follow up on the names you accumulated in Tactic #45, or use other sources to identify two or three influential or recognized people in your area. Then call them and set up a personal meeting at which you can get to know the person and obtain support, information, and referral to potential employers.

COMPLETION CHECK

5. COMMUNICATE YOUR RELEVANT PROBLEM-SOLVING ABILITIES TO THE APPROPRIATE POWER SOURCE IN A WAY THAT GETS HIM OR HER IN TOUCH WITH THE VALUE WHICH YOU OFFER

HELLO, I'M NOT HERE

We are engulfed in the hardware of communications. We have at our fingertips the most elaborate and advanced technologies ever conceived to move information around: telephones, television, AM and FM, message switching, TWX, microwaves, lasers, satellites, and all the endless products of the publishing and entertainment industries. And still it is almost impossible to get a clear answer to a simple question.

It is obvious that bigger and more complex communications systems have not contributed to a better understanding between people, whether they be parent/child, teacher/student, boss/subordinate, or job seeker/employer. As a matter of fact, with so much information flowing back and forth, it is virtually impossible to hear yourself above the noise.

Employers and job counselors are agreed that the one area in which most job seekers make the poorest showing is ability to communicate. Of course, applicants are pretty well agreed that the people who can't communicate well are the employers and job counselors.

What is true is that little of what goes on in the employment process (or in life on the job) is grounded in effective communication. When we review videotapes of employment interviews, for example, what we find is:

Questions which were never answered
Wasted words, taking too long, saying too little
Automatic, careless conversation
Wandering from subject to subject
People not listening
Time taken up with irrelevancies
People not asking directly for the thing they want to know
People only "hearing" the things they already agree with
Applicants not communicating value, but primarily demonstrating their needs

WHAT IS COMMUNICATION?

We are so deep in the middle of the communication process that we take it for granted. We never challenge the process itself. At workshops and lectures we often ask the attendees to give their answers to the question: *What is communication?* Here are some replies. (As you read them, think to yourself which, if any, *you* feel describes, or defines communication.)

Transmitting information
Expressing your feelings
Talking
Understanding another
Telling someone something
Relating to someone
Observing nonverbal signals
Knowing what you want to say, and saying it
Listening

What would you add to the description above? Take a few moments to answer the question from your own experience: *What is communication?* If you have a piece of paper handy, write your answer down; then look at it and see if it is adequate to describe your experience of communicating.

WHAT IT ISN'T

Talking is not communication: it's just talking. As a matter of fact, if we reduced the amount of talking we did, we would probably experience a marked increase in our communications. When you examine people's verbal dialogues in work and social settings you realize that most talking conveys very little information, is not connected to any clearly defined purpose, and accomplishes very little except to reinforce or remind people of each other's presence. If you mentally step back and observe people at a party or business conference you will begin to see that most of the chatter that goes back and forth is, essentially, without purpose.

We are talking machines: Jane tells Steve about her skiing trip to Aspen. While Jane is talking, Steve is thinking about his trip to Mount Snow, and deciding what he will say when Jane is finished. When Steve gets to tell his story, Jane is thinking about what she will say to top Steve's story and bring the subject back to herself. After 20 minutes of this the parties separate, and within a quarter of an hour neither knows much, if anything, of what the other party experienced. Little was accomplished in the verbal ping-pong match.

The same noncommunication often occurs in interviews: an unprepared interviewer asks a question, while the applicant is answering it, instead of listening, the interviewer is anxiously thinking up the next question. Job seekers, not sure of their footing or preoccupied with their own thoughts, frequently miss important clues in an employer's statements, or do not recognize the real questions underlying the superficial questions of an interviewer.

WHAT, THEN, IS COMMUNICATION?

Communication is the process of being responsible for ensuring that a message is received or recreated.

Read that aloud, and then follow through the elements below.

. . . THE PROCESS OF . . .

Real communication is not automatic. The process takes development, feedback, correction, and adaptation. You must be willing to realize where you are not effective, and expand and improve on those areas.

. . . BEING RESPONSIBLE . . .

This is the key element. A real communicator does what is necessary to get the message received. Most people blame others for not having received their communication: "He never listens," or "She's too stupid," or "You can't talk with anyone over there." This irresponsible approach to communication is like a pilot blaming the wind for his poor landing.

. . . FOR ENSURING . . .

A first step in the communication process is to determine what you need to do to get the communication through. If the other party is asleep, waken them first, rather than blame them for not getting it. If the other person doesn't get your message take a look at where you failed to penetrate the resistance. Then correct.

... THAT A MESSAGE IS RECEIVED

The message is received when the intended party can *re-create* is exactly. That is, if it were repeated back, it would all be there. A message is not necessarily received just because it is transmitted. If you tell an interviewer the details of an accomplishment that you feel was relevant, you may find that only part of the story got through. By obtaining good feedback you will be able to find out what has been received, and what has not. You can then repeat or paraphrase what was missed.

As we said, communication is a *process*.

THE 100% RULE

You are 100% responsible for your communication. It is not a 50-50 deal where you get to blame some other person, event, or set of circumstances for your lack of results.

In the 100% game you tell how well you communicated from what the other person "gets." If it isn't what you aimed for, you know you need to take corrective action. Be willing to admit it when you don't communicate. In the game of responsible communication, from your point of view the other party has zero responsibility for getting what you want to communicate. You have all of it, and must play from this position. It's 100% to 0%, and you are never the other party.

LISTENING AND HEARING

The flip side of the rule is that *as a listener or receiver of communications you are also 100% responsible*. Yes we know that appears contradictory. How can you be 100% responsible as a sender of communications and also be 100% responsible as a receiver? Because what you are totally responsible for is the context of the communications. You must be willing to do whatever you need to do to ensure that communication happens.

If you miss your mark, so what! Just go back again. Correct your aim and repeat the communication, or if you are the receiver, ask for the statement to be repeated or restated.

It is virtually impossible for most of us to hear exactly what is being said by another party. We miss the nuances and the subtext; the inarticulated assumptions. In training workshops where interviews are videotaped and played back for review, managers and supervisors who have considered themselves accomplished interviewers are often shocked to see how much they have missed hearing or seeing.

It has long been known in psychological circles that people tend to hear what they want to hear. We pick out of a conversation those things which tend to justify or support our own biases or stereotypes.

It has been observed by Werner Erhard and other authorities on the communication process that the mind is constantly subverbalizing. A "little voice in the head" is constantly judging and evaluating what is in front of it, shuffling hundreds of generally unrelated thoughts, ideas, pictures, suggestions, and reasons, forming an active voice-over on top of our apparent purpose.

Right now, without thinking further about it, close your eyes and, without effort, listen to the voice in your head for a few moments. Go ahead! Do it.

What did you get? Probably the first thing that came up was the question: "What voice?" That was it.

Stop again, and this time, with your eyes open, take a moment to observe the voice-over you carry around in your head.

This mind chatter goes on all the time at conscious, subconscious, and unconscious levels. It is always there—in everyone. There is nothing you can do to stop it. All you can do is acknowledge that it is there and still do whatever is necessary to receive another's communication. Recognize when your mind wanders, when you don't understand something or when you miss a point, and clear it up. "Would you mind asking that again? I didn't get it," is a perfectly acceptable way to clear up missed communications—in your work search and in your personal communications too.

TACTIC #48

Start to monitor your communication during social conversations or business discussions with co-workers and friends. Observe the voice in your head evaluating and judging and pulling your attention from the content of the communication. Also notice how much unnecessary information you add, and how it dilutes the clarity of what you are attempting to convey. Since it is very difficult to remember to watch your communication, try this: carry a small polished stone or small solid metal object in your pocket for a few weeks. Every time you feel it or see it, use that experience as a trigger device to remind you to observe your communications.

COMPLETION CHECK ☐

In the present application you are using good communications to present a particular problem-solving skill, or set of skills, to potential employers in a way that allows them to see how they will benefit from your skill. To accomplish this most powerfully, you must rehearse the key lines and phrases which most clearly convey the idea you wish to get. Some rules to follow:

- Have a clear idea of the results you wish to produce.
- Prepare key phrases in advance and list them on 3 x 5 cards. Know thoroughly the points you wish to make, but don't read them or repeat them from memory.
- Use direct action words to lead into accomplishments and results. Avoid lengthy windups and introductions.
- If possible, refer to some specific past achievement which will support and add credibility to your promised benefit.
- Give the person you are talking with the opportunity to get your communication. Don't rush; pause to allow questions.

TACTIC #49

With a tape recorder at hand, identify a real or imagined employer prospect in your job target field. Get a good mental picture of what he or she is looking for, and then turn on the tape. Ask yourself the question, Why should I hire you? and then answer it into the tape. Repeat the process three times giving different answers and then play the tape back, and listen to it as an employer. See how you the candidate communicated to you, the employer. What benefits did you communicate?

COMPLETION CHECK [ ]

THE EMPLOYMENT TRIANGLE

There are three parties to the hiring negotiations. You are one. The employing organization is another. The third party is the particular individual who interviews and makes, or influences, the hiring decision. The motivations of these three parties may not, indeed probably will not, be the same.

It would be naive to suppose a level of personal disinterestedness which would enable the hiring authority to hire the "best" person for the job regardless of personal likes or dislikes. Frankly, in all of the many hundreds of hours we have put in with employment interviewers, we have met very few (there *are* some) who are big enough to put aside personal fears, jealousies, role models, biases, and stereotypes. Remember how difficult it is for *you* to put aside this psychological baggage.

So don't be so dead set on the value and benefit which you feel you can provide for the employer that you ride with hobnail boots over the human on the other side of the desk. Before you go charging in with your rhetoric, find out enough from research, from the reaction to your initial contact, or from a well-planted discovery question at the beginning of the communication to avoid making the person feel that you are just a fast talker.

Don't threaten the interviewer. Don't give the impression that you are going to come racing in with the solutions to all the problems that he or she has been trying to solve for years. Don't expect people to hire their own replacement voluntarily unless they are very very secure.

Your communication to a potential boss or coworker should make it clear, as should your subsequent behavior, that if you are on the team, the team will win, and that one of your primary objectives is to make the boss win. *Bosses love to win*, and if they are clear that their relationship with you will allow them to experience their own victories, then you will find the universal hiring rule working at full power in the direction of good job offers for you.

The universal hiring rule is a statement of reality. It is the way things work. It is the logical method of making an offer the employer can't refuse.

REMINDERS AND REFERENCES

Reminders

- Name one thing that you can do better than anyone else you know.
- THE UNIVERSAL HIRING RULE: *Any employer will hire any individual so long as the employer is convinced that it will bring more value than it costs.*
- Real communication is being responsible for ensuring that a message is received or re-created.

References

Reflections on Language by Noam Chomsky. Pantheon, New York, 1976.

Word Play by Peter Farb. Bantam Books, New York, 1975.

Body Language by Julius Fast. Pocket Books, Division of Simon & Schuster, New York, 1971.

Suggestion: Learn to expand your ability to communicate—do workshops for verbal and non-verbal skills. Get feedback—listen to tapes of yourself.

Especially recommended—The *est* Communications Workshops. For details, write: *est*, 765 California Street, San Francisco, California 94108.

8

THE WAY IN

CHECKPOINT

Whether you are reading this book in anticipation of redirecting your worklife, to increase your store of life skills against a rainy day, or as a validation of what you already know, it's time to take a look at what you have accomplished at this stage, particularly if you have been doing the tactics.

In chapter 1 we looked at your worklife from the new context of work as an opportunity to express yourself in a way which creates satisfaction and aliveness for you and contributes value to others. We put you in touch with some updated ideas of what success is and how to have your worklife support your life working. You had the opportunity to begin to see how you could fit into the new, unpublicized work revolution.

In chapter 2 you took a voyage inward to look at basic problem-solving skills that are uniquely yours and at the personal interests which could be combined with your skills to uncover new directions in jobs. You saw that work can satisfy the hedonist in you as well as the puritan. You saw how people can make more money by doing work that turns them on.

In chapter 3 we made a quick survey of the development of jobs historically and into the 1980s. We gave you some insights into how jobs are actually created and some tools for staying on top of change and for increasing your value (and paycheck) in the expanding work game.

In chapter 4 the focus shifted to specific job targeting. There were tactics to relate your interests and skills to real jobs that represent you. You learned how to keep in touch with job growth and development in a variety of areas, and how to create valuable personal contacts and learn about work opportunities in other towns and overseas.

THE WAY IN

In chapter 5 you saw how the nature of education and training is changing along with the nature of work, and we showed you a variety of educational opportunities that can be tapped into as part of your worklife plan.

In chapter 6 we took you inside the hidden job market where 85% of the available jobs on a given day can be found, and showed you how to tap into these jobs through job market research.

In chapter 7 we revealed the universal hiring rule, the enormously successful approach to communicating value which most job seekers rarely get in touch with. We gave you some new ways to deal with your communications, not only in your worklife but every day.

In each chapter you have had the opportunity to go beyond the printed word and bring yourself into the picture. You have had the choice of using the book as a tool to support your growth in an evolving worklife or simply as interesting reading without involvement. Either position is a valid use of the material; however, if you get inside the process and engage the gears, you will make the material real for yourself. You do this by being willing to continually participate in the specific tactics, either as you go through the book or the second time through.

There is an immense personal and practical value to be gained by using the tactics in this book to clarify your own ideas and attitudes about your worklife, especially if you are willing to confront the reluctance which comes up along the way. It is not at all uncommon to experience some resistance to challenging this aspect of your life. We get so comfortable with a particular pattern that we prefer to repeat it even when it doesn't represent our ideals.

At this stage it is important to get in touch with the barriers which get in the way of your progress. You are now reaching the stage (if you are doing the tactics this time around) where you will move from the introspective and research phase into the action phase of your campaign. You are ready to start contacting people to set up meetings, and you will soon be taking part in interviews, following up to get offers, negotiating a salary, making phone calls, meeting experts. You will be out in the world and in the game. Use the following tactic to crystallize what you have achieved to date and to discover what barriers have been getting in the way.

TACTIC #50

Get in touch with your resistance to taking action in your job campaign. List five action steps that you now see are necessary in your job campaign (making phone calls, seeing people, asking for interviews, etc.). Under each, indicate the barriers or reasons you have found to avoid taking this action. Now list specific things you can do to overcome your resistance.

COMPLETION CHECK ☐

TARGETS, RÉSUMÉ, ACTION!

It has been our experience with thousands of job seekers that a job-finding campaign without the foundation of good personal life planning and job targeting is a waste of time. Job seekers end up getting into areas which don't interest them and which are dead ends for personal development and growth.

It is a mistake when facing a job change or a new job to simply sit down, crank a sheet of paper into the typewriter, bang out a résumé, have it reproduced, and mail out scores of copies. It is also a mistake to do all the introspective work, research dozens of work areas, uncover the names of potential employers, and then lean back and wait for opportunity to knock. It won't. *Opportunity does not knock!*

A well-managed worklife campaign has two different aspects to it: *research* and *action*. Research without action is like a well-planned military campaign where the troops forget to fire. Action without research brings the troops storming to their feet and running off in different directions. Both action and research are required.

THE WAY IN

This chapter brings you to the action stage in your own job search campaign.

It is the time in the job search process when you first put yourself in a position to be rejected. *Rejected!* The word sends a shiver down everyone's spine. We all have a serious problem about feeling rejected, turned down, put off, ignored, passed over, told "NO." It doesn't matter who you are, the negative power of a potential rejection is virtually universal.

It's valuable here to reinforce the picture which we drew earlier of a typical job campaign. Regardless of who you are, what your level, your discipline, your age, sex, or race is, the standard job campaign looks like this:

NO NO NO NO NO NO NO NO
NO NO NO NO NO NO NO *YES*

That's exactly the way it is. The job campaign, by its very nature, consists of people not being in, not returning your calls, not inviting you back, not wanting to talk to you, and so forth. What you must know in advance is that NO is what you should expect, and that this is not a comment on your worth as a human. *Rejection is a basic part of the employment process.* The way to get your campaign really going is to *accelerate* the speed at which you are told no. Literally get the nos to happen faster. Feel excited and rewarded when you knock three more nos off the list! You are that much closer to the Yes.

TACTIC #51

Keep a record of the first 10 or 20 turndowns, rejections, or refusals which you get. After each, list your feelings and emotions. Also write down what you see to be the net practical effect on your job campaign. What behavior does it tend to inhibit? Are you willing to transcend these inhibitions and create results in your job campaign?

COMPLETION CHECK

It's worthwhile to stay with this general discussion of the coming direct action phase of your career life plan a little longer, since this is an area where most of us get stuck. Your assertive step out into the world with your new career direction, your new job targets, your realization of the potential for work satisfaction, and your hopes, can change to a timid retreat if you aren't willing to handle the inevitable disappointments along the path.

It can be tough to go after what you want in the adult world. Our child selves keep coming through hoping that someone will do it for us. Uncle Sam will take care of it all. Perhaps the school guidance counselor has the answer. Perhaps the job we are in isn't that bad after all. Maybe we should listen to the employment agent.

The temptations to quit the game can be severe, and deceptive. When there is something you don't really want to face, the world conveniently comes up with a lot of reasons for you to put it off: there isn't enough time this month, there's a vital project at home, the winter doesn't seem like the best time, you deserve a short vacation, probably you should wait until the kids get a little older. The list is endless.

Doug Harlon

I was a zombie for about a year. Literally, my energy was sapped by my indecisiveness and my unwillingness to do what I knew had to be done. I don't mind telling you now that this period of my job change was one of the most difficult of my entire life.

The fact that I had just turned 35 didn't help. Even though I was 35, not 65, I felt old and helpless, and ready to give up my best intentions and opportunities.

The whole thing started around a year ago, when I got a promotion. I had worked for this promotion for two years, and guess I had a rather inflated idea of what it would be. The small increase in salary I got was an insult. At least that's what I thought then. I wasn't that happy with the job anyway, so I decided to change. The decision really felt good, like a big load lifted off my shoulders.

THE WAY IN

Once I had made up my mind to leave there wasn't any way that I could be happy where I was.

After I went to the career workshop, I became very motivated by the possibilities. In a burst of self-confidence, I told my boss that I would probably be leaving in five or six months and that I would help him find and train a replacement before I got relocated. I agreed to take vacation days for any time I used for interviews. Some people say I was crazy to tell him, but I know that if I hadn't I might still be there. The fact that he knew kept some pressure on me.

Choosing the job targets was easy. I did the process in the workshop and I was excited about the target I came up with: internal risk management for a major insurance firm in the New England area. To an outsider that might not sound too exciting, but to someone in the field it has meaning.

I did all the exercises, laid out my job targets, prepared a résumé, and was well into the research phase after a few weeks. My wife, Gerry, was helping me and everything was going well.

Next I had an interview arranged through a friend with one of the big insurance companies in Hartford, a perfect place for what I wanted to do. I was absolutely certain they would be anxious to hire me. I felt as if I had been thrown in with sharks. I was interviewed by three executives at the same time, the toughest interview I have ever had. I forgot everything I ever knew. They told me very bluntly at the end that I wasn't what they were looking for. Just like that. I was knocked back hard. I got depressed and stayed away for several weeks. It wasn't a really heavy depression, it was more of a fear, and it was clearly related to my career. Perhaps I might not make it.

Ever since school I had pretty much achieved what I wanted. I had been a Marine Corps pilot after school, gotten three good offers from management training programs, received two raises with the firm I was with, and had married a beautiful, intelligent woman. It had all come easily, and now I was terrified.

I felt immobilized when it came to taking

everything I had learned out into the actual workworld, and the longer I took, the more nervous I became. I thought of changing my mind if Charlie, my boss, would let me. Anything but make those calls.

One Monday, I stayed home and made four calls. Score: two were not in, one turned me down, one asked to be sent a résumé. This didn't help. I went into a holding pattern. We didn't talk much about the job campaign. Occasionally my boss would remind me. I don't think he had anyone special in mind, but he kept reminding me that I was going. I didn't quite know how to take it. I still don't.

Finally, Terry got me through it. She set up a schedule, got me to agree to it, and then kept me going during the day until I had *completed* ten calls. Six hours it took. I had gotten three people interested, one seriously, and two would look at my résumé. The serious one actually set up an interview. What this meant was that anytime I wanted another interview I could get one by being willing to put in six hours of calling, and I got it down to an average of one interview for every four hours I was willing to call. It was no longer important that people said No. I knew that all I needed to do was make some more calls and a Yes would be there.

My interviews were transformed. I no longer had such a dependency on any particular organization, there were more where they came from, so I came across more confidently. I developed a skill in making calls that I will never lose. No fear of phoning here.

The new job is in Philadelphia. We had to move, and we both loved it. I will no longer be stymied in my career. I broke through the barrier.

WHO DO YOU KNOW

You know someone who knows someone who can get you an introduction to almost any employer you want to see.

- Your cousin Janice went to school with a man who is now a banker and has access to many of the financial organizations you are trying to contact.

THE WAY IN

- Your ex-husband has as a customer the head of one of the city's top ad agencies. This person could undoubtedly get you some introductions at the local newspapers for your job target as a copy editor.
- Your college placement director knows several managers at the local IBM division and can give you the name of someone to call.
- The congressman you helped campaign for can reach by phone any employer in town, and will do so if properly approached.
- Your wife's co-board members on the PTA are in touch with many executives, among them several in organizations you wish to contact.

Most people's initial response to uncovering personal referrals is that they think they don't know anyone who could help. With a little probing it becomes obvious that the problem is not that they don't know anyone, but that they've been very restrictive in the people they are willing to approach in their job search.

Allow your friends to support and assist you in your job search. Insist on it. Don't be heroic, don't try to deal with the world single-handed. The bad news is that it takes at least two to really make it. The more support you can create for yourself the further you will go. Don't believe it? Observe the people in your life who are really producing results, and around them you will see an army of support, paid and unpaid. Powerful people are supported by others.

Some embarrassment creeps in when people start to think about letting others know that they are in the job market and looking for leads. You may not want to look as if you have a problem, but you *do* have a problem. Everyone else has the same problem, and the same opportunity for a solution. How can we focus our resources in a way which allows us to make a major contribution and achieve satisfaction at the same time? Peter Drucker, in his book *The Effective Executive* (Harper & Row), comments: "Individual self-development in large measure depends upon the focus on contribution."

TEST

If you want to know how your friends will react to your request for assistance in your job campaign, try the following test: Imagine a specific person whom you would consider calling, *calling you* on the phone and saying: "I'm calling to ask if you would do something for me. I'm thinking of possibly switching careers and want to explore some ideas in the area of bookselling. I know that you were involved in that field for a while, and I wonder if you would give me the names of some people I could call to get information."

How did you react? Would you cooperate? Do you feel imposed upon? Do you feel your friend is "in trouble"? We doubt it. Try this one (coming to you from a stranger): "Helen Levine suggested that I call you as she feels that you are very experienced and qualified in the area of computers. I've just completed a course in programming, and am looking for leads in banking where I might uncover some opportunities to put my skills to work. Could you give me the name of a good employment agency in this field? And perhaps you also know some people who manage computer facilities."

Our guess is that when approached by someone else you feel no threat. You want to help. People want to help you. People are *very* willing to give information if they are acknowledged and treated with respect and consideration.

TACTIC #52

List five specific tasks or problems which you feel you could be assisted in by others. Then list two people from your support system who could assist you in accomplishing these tasks or problems. Are you willing to approach these people for their assistance?

COMPLETION CHECK

THE PERFECT RÉSUMÉ

Fallacy: A good résumé will get you the job you want.
Fallacy: Your résumé will be read carefully and thoroughly by an interested party.
Fallacy: The purpose of the résumé is to list your skills and abilities.
Fallacy: The more good information you present about yourself in your résumé the better.
Fallacy: If you want a really good résumé, you should have it prepared professionally.

Fact: Hundreds of thousands of unsolicited résumés cross employers' desks each and every working day.
Fact: Your résumé probably has under ten seconds to make an initial impression.
Fact: Most résumés, at every employment level, do not communicate clearly.
Fact: A majority of résumés actually do a disservice to the job seeker.
Fact: You should have a perfect résumé.

The résumé is a specific, written, directed communication with one very clear purpose: *to present your accomplishments in a way which so clearly demonstrates your ability to produce results in an area of interest to a potential employer that she or he becomes interested in meeting you personally.*

Let's tune in again to our panel of employment experts, and see what they have to say in answer to our question:

"What are the most common faults in the résumés you see?"

> Employer No. 1: "I read hundreds of résumés each week, and I must say that there are very few that are clear. I have to dig to find out what I need to know."
>
> Employer No. 2: "Too much meaningless redundant information. Most are poorly written and too long."

Employer No. 3: "Maybe one out of every five résumés I receive is what I would call intelligently prepared with a clear sense of organization. The balance hardly get read, let alone considered."

Employer No. 4: "Much of the information appears irrelevant or unclear. I can't relate it to what we are looking for.

Employer No. 5: "I would suggest that applicants spend less time mailing out dozens of résumés, and more time making the ones they do send out relate clearly to practical requirements."

A perfect résumé is like proper attire for a job interview: If you are not properly dressed, you certainly *won't* get the job. However, the fact that you *are* well dressed doesn't guarantee an offer.

The biggest problem associated with résumés, in our experience, is that applicants frequently use the résumé as a substitute for a job campaign. They will put lots of time and attention into it, print up 300 copies, mail them out, and then sit around and hope for responses. This waiting time will get them into trouble if they are using it to avoid handling the next steps in their job campaign. Procrastination is the enemy, because the longer you wait without accomplishing movement in your work search, the lower your energy and intention will be.

RÉSUMÉ RULES

Rule 1: *Know Your Reader*. Picture a tired recruiter faced with a pile of 50 résumés and a busy day filled with a myriad of other duties. Your résumé is stuck somewhere in the middle of the pile. This is your audience. Your résumé will only have a few precious seconds to make a first impression. The recruiter has no interest in figuring out what you are trying to say or probing beneath the surface for hidden skills which you have not clearly communicated. If your message is clear and well organized, and communicates direct, relevant value, you may get a more thorough appraisal. If not, a form rejection will be on its way to you.

Rule 2: *Take Inventory*. Don't start your résumé until you have listed your skills and accomplishments. Record on a large sheet of paper everything you can think of which has produced measurable results. This prewritten inventory will serve as a resource from which you can pick and choose the most relevant aspects of your background to use in your résumé for a particular job target. (You will generally want to use a different résumé for each *major* job target area, up to a maximum of three or four résumés, no more.) Don't write your résumé until you have completed this inventory.

Rule 3: *Select the Appropriate Format*. Résumés are typically organized along one of three common formats —each with a particular purpose and strength.

CHRONOLOGICAL FORMAT

In this format, experience and accomplishments are organized by employer worked for, starting with the most recent and work backward to the earliest since completion of your schooling. Dates, titles, and employers are shown as a lead into each major time block. The most recent employment experience, unless very brief, takes up the most space. If more than three or four jobs are represented, the earlier ones can be lumped together to avoid repetition.

The *advantages* of the chronological résumé are that it highlights the most recent experience, is easy to follow, and is most widely used and understood.

The *disadvantage* is that it will tend to call attention to a spotty employment record and stress recent experience, which may be a hindrance if you are planning to change fields. It will also highlight any lack of experience.

FUNCTIONAL FORMAT

In the functional résumé, you do not organize the accomplishments according to dates, but under functional or topical headings. The functional area in which you have the most personal interest is at the top, followed by at least two other functions (design, production, office management, purchasing, retailing, etc.). You do not include identification of employers or dates, as these are secondary in this approach, which allows you to camouflage an irrelevant or poor work record.

The *advantage* of the functional résumé is that you get to organize your background in accordance with your own ideas of the relative values in your life, and stress areas of experience and interest in which you might never have held down a regular job.

The *disadvantage* is that the résumé can be suspected of hiding information and, since dates and employers are not given, it can be confusing. For people reentering the job market or going after their first position, it can be ideal.

COMBINED FORMAT

The combined résumé format is a functional résumé with a synopsis chronology of employers and dates and places worked. It provides advantages from each of the first two résumé types listed, and is highly recommended for anyone following the self-directed job search discussed in this book.

The *advantage* of the combined résumé is that it enables you to organize and present your accomplishments so as to support your selected job target and to maximize your impact in this area even if you don't have much directly related experience. This ability to organize your presentation according to your interests rather than your past work experience is very valuable if you are changing career fields, or going after your first job.

The *disadvantages* are that this format is not as logical as the chronological approach and tends to play down your direct experience with specific employers.

CHRONOLOGICAL RESUME

JACK DEUTSCH
4115 Sommer Road
Warwick, New York
(914) 968-6351

EXPERIENCE:

12/75 - Present   GOODSON APPAREL INDUSTRIES, INC.
                  New York, New York

Divisional Controller

Reported directly to the chief financial officer. Managed cash funds, prepared consolidated corporate tax returns for seven companies and financial review of major subsidiaries. Designed and prepared a monthly sales comparison report for corporate executives. Co-supervisor of a twelve-member staff that handled all facets of accounting for a 25-million-dollar company.

10/74 - 12/75   MACY'S INC.
                New York, New York

Corporate Auditor

Reported directly to the Assistant Corporate Controller. Conducted operational and financial audits within the Treasurer's office and five operating divisions. Developed a report with findings and recommendations for the chief executive officer of each division and numerous management personnel.

6/67 - 10/74   PRICE, WATERHOUSE & COMPANY
               Certified Public Accountants
               New York, New York

Supervising Senior

Joined the professional staff as an assistant accountant. Reported directly to partners and managers. Planned, supervised and completed numerous audit assignments.

AWARDS, ACCREDITATIONS, AND MEMBERSHIPS:

Peter K. Ewald Award in Taxation - June, 1967; Certified Public Accountant, New York State - April, 1971; American Institute of Certified Public Accountants; New York State Society of Certified Public Accountants.

EDUCATION:

Hofstra University - B.S. in Accounting - June, 1967

FUNCTIONAL RESUME

MARTIN ERHARD
4220 Seacliff Avenue
St. Louis, Missouri 63125

BUSINESS: Publicity coordinator for a service organization. Responsibilities included analyzing, writing and approving press releases, planning and directing public relations activities, and negotiating and managing the budget.

Created and developed a marketing audit for an organization designed to improve the overall efficiency and effectiveness of the institution.

Elected treasurer for a self-help organization. Duties included balancing the books and approving and issuing checks.

NUTRITION: Read over 150 publications in the field of nutrition.

Took a course in nutrition at the University.

Created and developed a total nutritional program for myself over a period of eighteen months. Research is continuing.

Currently employed with Green House Health Food Corp. managing the vitamin annex, ordering inventory, selling vitamins and answering questions.

EDUCATION: B.S. in Business Administration, Washington University 1977, Cum Laude.

COMBINATION RESUME

ELLEN MESINE
2217 Sepulveda Blvd.
San Francisco, California 94310

SALES MANAGEMENT:

<u>Sales Representative:</u> Planned and implemented phone, mail and public sales presentations that increased business 30%. Developed and led over 100 presentations in the U.S. and Mexico to over 1,000 people.

<u>Conference Service Manager:</u> Booked 17 local and national conferences within 3 months. Initiated and researched conference sales campaign. Created multimedia sales presentation. Negotiated all fees and contracts; supervised staff of 20 in handling all conference services.

PROMOTION/ADVERTISING:

Introduced successful promotional phone campaigns to create magazine articles, newspaper coverage and radio interviews. Worked with artists, writers, photographers and layout people to create initial promotional material. Promoted college horsemanship program to full capacity first semester.

PROGRAM DEVELOPER:

Created, developed and managed horsemanship programs for children and college students. Directed women's center; initiated counseling services and special courses. Co-developed newsletter for over 1,000 readers. Responsible for designing and delivering training sessions for 10 - 150 people.

EXPERIENCE:

1975 - 1977
Fox Forest Resort, Reno, Nevada
Conference Service Manager/Sales Representative.

California State University, Petaluma, Calif.
Director of Horsemanship Program, Department of Physical Education.

1973 - 1975
Management Consultants, Inc. San Diego, Calif.
Head, Department of Enrollment - Assistant to President.

1972 - 1973
Administrative Assistant of Los Angeles Womens Center, Los Angeles, California.

EDUCATION:
Riverside High School	1971
Claremont Business School 2-yr accreditation	1973

TACTIC #53

Reread the advantages and disadvantages of the chronological, functional, and combined résumé formats. Then analyze your own needs and objectives, and decide which format will best represent you.

COMPLETION CHECK ☐

Rule 4: *Present Your Accomplishments.* Let the potential employer know about your past accomplishments which could relate to his needs, not just the job titles you have had or the duties you were supposed to perform. People can comprehend tangible results far easier than sterile-sounding job descriptions or duties. Use quantities and specifics to create a picture of what you produced. Consult the lists you created in tactic no. 42 and select the accomplishments which are most relevant to the job target represented by the résumé. Incorporate them in your résumé.

Rule 5: *Start with Action.* Begin sentences and paragraphs with verbs which convey actions, such as:

Designed	Directed	Organized
Produced	Managed	Edited
Started	Controlled	Built
Researched	Sold	Learned

Don't beat around the bush. Don't use long windups. Communicate your abilities and your accomplishments directly. The more you bury your real talents in a maze of qualifiers and connectives, the less they will be recognized.

Your writing style should be more terse than descriptive. Edit out extra words and phrases which repeat points you have already made. Strange as it may seem, the more you repeat (in a résumé), the less clear the communication is.

Don't use fancy or cute writing styles unless you are in a field where this is acknowledged as appropriate.

Rule 6: *Keep Your Résumé to One Page.* This is the length most employers prefer; it communicates the most information per unit of reading time. And you can do it! There are very few people whose entire career cannot be described clearly in one page. Please try it. If you have a lot of publications or projects to list, put them in a separate addendum, but present your primary selling message on one neatly organized page.

Rule 7: *Make a Rough Draft First.* Do not attempt to produce a finished résumé on the first pass, or you will probably represent your abilities poorly. What follows is a proved procedure for developing a résumé.

1. Decide whether you will use a chronological, functional, or combined résumé format.

2. Get a separate sheet of paper (preferably legal size) for each function you plan to include—or each position you plan to discuss, if you are using the chronological format. List a separate function or position at the top of each sheet. Then draw a line across the sheet one-third of the way up from the bottom. You are now ready to start writing.

3. On the top two-thirds of the sheet write down *everything* you can think of related to that function or particular job. Pour out as much information as you can, related to your accomplishments on the job and other relevant skills and duties. Don't worry about organization or structure at this point, but don't write on the bottom one third of the sheet.

4. After you have written on the top of the paper everything you can think of related to each skill or function, go back over it and underline the most powerful, least redundant, most descriptive statements, those that you would want to include in your résumé. Then use the bottom third of each sheet to rewrite the key information on that function or position, condensing and writing clearly and powerfully.

5. After you have written a very tight paragraph for

each function or position, cut these paragraphs from the sheets and position them in order on top of a fresh sheet of paper with tape or a stapler. This will allow you to have an overview of everything you want to include and let you see how it all works together. You can also see how long the résumé is and whether you have to cut it to fit on one page. Leave room at the top of this sheet to list your name, address, phone number, and education.

6. Now write a fresh new draft from the information you have organized so far. Cut and edit as appropriate to fit on one page.

Rule 8: *Eliminate Extraneous Information.* After you have drafted your résumé, go over it again to eliminate extraneous information. Take out everything that does not directly present your accomplishments in a way which clearly demonstrates your ability to produce results. You should *leave out* most of the following information:

Age and sex
Height and weight
Hobbies and awards (unless related to job target)
Race or religion
Military service (unless it was a career)
Part-time jobs
References
Your objective or desired title (restrict this to the cover letter to keep the résumé flexible)
Salary
Reasons for leaving last job
Any self-evaluating or self-serving statement (such as "I am a good leader" or "I am very dependable")

Rule 9: *Have It Critiqued.* Once you have prepared a draft of your résumé, you must get someone to go over it. If possible, find someone with experience in reviewing résumés: a personnel manager, a recruiter, a placement counselor, or someone with experience in your field. Be sure to set it up so that you will get real feedback, not just approval. Don't ask: "Say, how do you like my résumé?" Instead say: "How do you think I can improve this?" and then *listen* to the feedback. Don't explain or justify what you have done. Here are some of the things that should be checked:

Spelling and grammar
Clarity and organization
Lack of redundancy
Basic layout
Presentation of accomplishments

You might want to ask the person who will critique your résumé to read this chapter first and then be as hard on you as possible. Obviously it's better to have someone critique the résumé before you send it out than have the employer do it when it's too late to change it.

Rule 10: *Make It Beautiful*. The appearance of your résumé is as important to your presentation as the way you dress is to your interview. If you are not a top-notch typist with a good, clean electric typewriter, have someone else do the final version. Make certain that the layout is attractive, with enough white space so that it is easy to read. Avoid overlong paragraphs and sentences. Use indentations and underlinings judiciously—don't overuse them. If you have a friend in personnel who reviews lots of résumés, have him select one or two layouts, which he feels are good, to give your typist as a guide. If you need assistance look in the Yellow Pages for professional typing services. (There is no need, by the way, to have your résumé *written* by someone else. Such a résumé often comes across as too slick. You should do the preparation and have a professional do the typing.)

Have your résumé offset printed on good quality white, buff, or ivory bond paper. Don't get into flamboyant colors or binders unless you are in a field where this is appropriate. Don't include a photograph on or with your résumé.

TACTIC #54

Set aside a five-hour period to produce an effective one-page, professional-looking résumé. Assemble any earlier résumés you have produced, and any other work references or resources which can help you.

Be willing to stay with an all-out concentrated effort which will result in a well-written, effective résumé. Use your support system to critique and assist you.

COMPLETION CHECK ☐

THE CUSTOM COVER LETTER

A well-done, individually prepared cover letter sent along with your résumé is almost equivalent to a personal introduction for an interview. It personalizes the communication in a way that the printed résumé could never do on its own.

It is our strong belief after over a dozen years of involvement with literally thousands of résumés and scores of employers, that a well-prepared custom cover letter will make a major difference in the number of interviews you get as a result of your résumé mailing.

The custom cover letter is a personal, individually typed (never offset or xeroxed) communication which should go out with every résumé you send. It is designed to relate the information about your background to the needs of a particular employer. Here are the rules for preparing a cover letter:

1. Each cover letter should be addressed to a specific person (the person who could hire you) by *name*.

2. Each cover letter should indicate, in the first sentence, something which will show the potential employer that you know something specific about his activities. This establishes that the letter is not a form letter.

3. In the opening paragraph you should state, or at least imply, that you are aware of what the organization needs or wants to accomplish. This does not need to be

highly researched information and can usually be based on your own common sense or general understanding of the field.

4. In the next paragraph you should communicate something about your background that could be valuable to the employer, particularly in relation to the implied problem of the opening paragraph. A simple statement of your ability or accomplishment with a reference to the appropriate section of your résumé is sufficient.

5. The final step in your cover letter is to request an interview at a specific time and place. By going after a specific interview date you help accelerate the decision-making process.

Shown on pages 210-211 are two examples of custom cover letters:

SAMPLE COVER LETTER

204 Palisade Street
Olympia, Washington 96403
Phone: 843-2971

Dr. Warren Stanton, President
Seattle Heights Junior College
12 Foxhollow Road
Seattle, Washington 98101

Dear Dr. Stanton:

My experience on the administrative staffs of two colleges should be of interest to you in your new drive to centralize administrative functions of SHJC.

The enclosed resume will illustrate my ability to handle the specific administrative problems of a college department.

I am moving to Seattle at the end of this school year. I will be in Seattle from April 10-14. If possible, I would like to arrange an appointment during that period to discuss your new organization, and how my experience could make a contribution to your program.

Yours very truly,

Christine Williams

Christine Williams

Encl. Resume

SAMPLE COVER LETTER

>1736 D. Street N.W.
>Washington, D.C. 20006
>(202) PO7-8192

Mr. Robert Olsen, President
Vendo Corporation
1742 Sunshine Drive
Fort Lauderdale, Florida

Dear Mr. Olsen,

I was intrigued by the write-up of your new portable vending centers as described in <u>Sales Management</u> magazine. Frankly, I think it is an extremely good idea.

As you will note from the enclosed resume, my market planning and sales management experience could be of great assistance to you at this early stage in your project.

Because of my familiarity with the types of locations and clients you are seeking, I am sure that if we were able to work together in this new venture, the results would reflect my contribution.

I have roughed out some specific marketing ideas which you might like to review, and would like to make arrangements to meet with you in Florida during the week of February 15th.

I am looking forward to meeting with you.

Very truly yours,

Leonard Hardwick

TACTIC #55

Write the first five cover letters to potential employers. Follow the steps outlined above, including some initial research about each potential employer. Continue this process of cover letter preparation through your campaign.

COMPLETION CHECK ☐

THE RÉSUMÉ ALTERNATIVE LETTER

There are several situations where it may not be appropriate to put together a standard résumé: for example, when you have no work experience, when you have been out of the labor force for a long time, or when you have had far too many job changes. In these cases, one approach which may work to get interviews is to write an expanded cover letter instead of a résumé.

To be effective, this résumé alternative letter requires more detailed research than the regular cover letter, to make it clear to the reader that you can contribute real value to his organization. The letter should also provide some additional information so that you can get by without the employer asking you to "send a résumé." It should mention education level (directly or indirectly), name, address and *telephone number*, and if possible the name of someone known to the employer, for credibility. You can sometimes use the name of someone even if the only conversation you have ever had was to call and ask him or her for job advice.

Above all, the résumé alternative letter should be clear about the specific benefit it promises or implies to the prospective employer. This will take research, at least three hours per employer. It's worth it if you have serious difficulty in putting together a résumé.

Here is a sample of the résumé alternative letter.

RESUME ALTERNATIVE

1011 Orange Court
Pasadena, California 92318
213/787-2724

Mr. Samuel H. Gruen
Medical Laboratories Limited
425 San Marco Blvd.
Pacific Dunes, California 92316

Dear Mr. Gruen,

Dr. Paul Benenson at the USC Graduate School suggested that I contact you about the studies your firm is currently making into the utilization of nursing homes in this country. He also remarked that you might be thinking about hiring someone to coordinate the field investigations which are part of your study.

As an officer of our local Women's Community Center, I have had a great deal of experience with the operation of day care centers, which, as you know, are quite similar administratively to nursing homes. This experience includes familiarity with the financial and administration aspects of the centers as well as knowledge of the programming and educational considerations. I have met with the staffs of most of the day care centers in the county, and am certain that my ability to work with these professionals would enable me to facilitate the execution of your study.

In addition to this experience, I have had two years of administrative work on any important research project in health care at USC while working on my master's degree in education.

I plan to be near your office next week and wonder if we could get together on Wednesday or Thursday for an interview. I'll call you to confirm when you will be available.

Yours truly,

Norma Delsey

A final reminder: Take the time to create a perfect résumé and use it. But don't fall into the trap of thinking that mass-mailed résumés constitute a job campaign. If you have enough money to do it effectively, go ahead and intelligently mail out 100 or 200 résumés. But keep in mind that this is only 25% of your job campaign. The rest of it must be direct, specific, and persistent. That's what really works.

TACTIC #56

Have your cover letter and résumés critiqued by a member of your support system, or by someone in a professional capacity in your job target area. Encourage them to give you as much correction as they can, without apology.

COMPLETION CHECK ☐

FIGHT PHONE FEAR

In the eyes of most job seekers the telephone is a small modern instrument designed to say no. People of competence in matters of great importance are often very reluctant to pick up the phone and call potential employers as job seekers. Normally talkative salesmen turn shy when they think their careers are on the line. Even telephone operators probably would rather mail résumés than to phone for interviews.

Telephoning strangers is considered by many to be hard sell at its worst. All the times we have been turned down for a date, refused admittance to a club, told that the flights were all filled, that a show was sold out, or that our daughter was not accepted by a private school are associated with the phone.

And yet, mastery of the telephone is essential to the success of your work search. The issue needs to be faced squarely and realistically: *Are you willing to make the calls necessary to your job search?* How many? No one can tell in advance. Be prepared to make a *minimum* of 50 to acquire a sense of the variety of opportunities available to you. And there is no maximum. You will set your own standards and reach for your own goals and targets. The fact is, *so long as you are willing to continue to make exploratory calls to potential employers and to communicate clearly and positively about your ability to provide value and benefit, you will connect to valuable work opportunities for yourself.*

This has been proved over and over and over again at every level. In a recent project in San Diego, California, hard-to-place, so-called "disadvantaged" persons, usually relegated to the employment reject bin, were put through an innovative training program run by Self Directed Placement, Inc., in which they were trained in job-finding and communications techniques, given phones and the Yellow Pages, and encouraged to make over 50 calls per day. The results: 81% of them obtained jobs within four weeks, an astonishing success when compared to that of the usual sit-around-and-wait approach.

Please keep a few things in mind:

- There are an unlimited number of people or employers to contact in fields which could satisfy your job goals. For example, here is a random selection of listings of names available from a rather typical direct mail broker (check your Yellow Pages for mailing list brokers):

Manufacturing firms	260,269
Management consultants	105,342
Cemeteries	10,080
Summer camps	6,725
Dentists	117,824
Greeting card stores	9,115
Interior decorators	17,400
Insurance executives	20,183
Lithographers	4,286

- If you are communicating a potential benefit rather than a need, three out of five people will talk to you when you call.

- When you receive a negative response, it is not directed to you *personally*, it's just part of the process which everyone goes through (NO NO NO NO NO ... remember?).
- If you organize your information in advance, you can easily *complete* 20 calls a day.
- The more calls you make, the more interviews you will get. The more interviews you get, the more job offers you will receive. The more offers you receive, the better job you can select, and the more money you will make.

Helpful hint: Do your research first, including the name of the person you wish to contact. List 25 (minimum) to 50 potential employers in each of your job target areas on 3 x 5 cards *before you start your calls*. Schedule your calling to begin at a particular time, preferably at 8:30 or 9:00 a.m. Set it up so that you are not interrupted or distracted. Call until you have reached five persons, then take a 15-minute break for a cup of coffee or a walk around the block. Recommence the calling promptly on schedule and continue until you have reached another five—and so forth through the day. Keep track of the time you start calling and when you end, and note what your results are in terms of the number of people reached per hour of calling. Also, note the results of each call on the card and, on a separate sheet of paper, critique yourself. Note how you could have improved the presentation.

TACTIC #57

Set up the time and space for your calling program. Allocate sufficient time for you to do the research to list at least 50 employers to call. Follow the instructions detailed above, and make your first 25 completed calls. Continue this procedure throughout your job campaign.

COMPLETION CHECK ☐

WHAT TO SAY

At this point in your job campaign you are interested in only one thing: *interviews*. You have done all of the preliminary work you need or wish to do. This is it. It is time to set up face-to-face visits with employer targets.

The message you need to communicate to the potential employer is, quite simply, that you have the potential for assisting him meet his objectives in a way that could be valuable both to his organization and to him personally. *In other words, you will bring him more value than cost.* (The universal hiring rule.)

Here are the steps that must be covered:

- Preparation: Before the call have a clear idea of who you are communicating to, by name and title, and what you want to say. Note this on the 3 x 5 card.
- When the person answers, assuming you get through directly, the first thing to establish is that she or he is the right one and that she or he has a few moments to talk. Don't rush into your spiel. Establish communication first.

    "Hello, Ms. Marks. This is Bob Rich, do you have a few moments?"

    If "No":

    "Fine, when would be a good time to call you back to talk to you about your new fisheries contract?"

    If "Yes":

    "Great, is it correct that you are taking over the new fisheries contract?"

- Then, within one minute, communicate something about yourself which you feel is directly related to a problem or need that the employer has.

    "I would imagine that this new contract will require people with good underwater photography experience. I have done some work in a very similar project and would like to meet (don't talk about interviews, talk about meetings) in order to show you how I might be able to help you with this contract."

- At this point, pause to allow the person on the other end of the line to have a reaction, to ask a question, or to raise an objection (see below). When this occurs, address yourself to the response, restating the main point you wish to make, the benefit you offer. If you note any annoyance or antagonism, don't respond to it argumentatively, simply "get it" and continue to communicate your support as clearly as possible.
- Establish credibility. If possible use the name of a person or organization you know the employer will recognize. Or use facts and figures to strengthen your short presentation.

> "I worked directly with Ann Seldenge, the director of the underwater research project, and together we developed a new technique."

- Never mention that you are looking, or have been looking, for a job. Avoid the temptation often displayed by nervous job seekers to lead with negative information: "I haven't worked for three years, but I would like to . . ." or "I don't know that much about —— but would be willing to find out." We're not telling you to lie, simply don't advertise the things you are worried about. You will have one minute to communicate a clear, *irresistible* value.
- Ask for a "meeting" (interview) at a specific time. Do this as lightly as possible, with the intimation that the employer could have a productive, enjoyable half hour with you. Eliminate the "need" from your voice.

> "It might be a good idea for us to get together next week when I could describe this in more detail. Are you free on Tuesday afternoon?"

or:

> "I would like to meet with you this week, if it's convenient, so we could explore this further. Are you available for coffee tomorrow morning?"

- Don't stop at the first NO. There is a popular sales motto which says, "The sale begins when the customer says No." Follow this. Realize that the initial response to almost any new proposition is negative. Allow the response to occur, then restate the benefits or answer the objection, clearly, and ask again for a meeting.

MEETING OBJECTIONS

Every step along the way in your job campaign you will meet resistance from others in the form of reasons why they can't do what you want or grant what you ask for.

These objections are an expected part of your job campaign. They are the rule, not the exception. They are virtually automatic. The majority of people, when confronted by an objection from another, will stop in their tracks, apologize, and back off. That is what you will want to do. Don't.

Here is how to handle an objection:

1. Get it. Don't pretend you didn't hear it or that it is untrue. Don't argue about the objection. Allow the person on the other end of the line to experience that you got it.

2. Respond to it with a clear communication of benefit or value that can overcome the objection without denying it.

3. Reintroduce the original request.

Here are some examples of what we mean:

YOU: I'd like to stop by to discuss this with you further.
THEM: Well, frankly, we're cutting back our staff now and don't have any openings.
YOU: I see, I can understand why you wouldn't want to talk now. On the other hand, I think that I could show you how to organize the project so as to get even more done with a smaller staff. Why not take 20 minutes to consider it? I could be there early tomorrow.

GUERRILLA TACTICS IN THE JOB MARKET

YOU: Would it be possible for us to meet next week?

THEM: I don't think so. You don't have the kind of experience we are looking for.

YOU: Yes. That's probably right. However, I think that the experience I do have could be very valuable to you in another way. If we could spend 20 minutes together, I could show you what I mean, and how I could probably make a major contribution to your department. Would you be willing to give me 20 minutes of your time to show you?

YOU: I think that my organizational skills could get your department to work even more efficiently than it does now.

THEM: I doubt that. You don't have any direct experience in our field.

YOU: That's true. And I don't mean to imply that your office isn't well organized. It's just that I feel I could make a valuable contribution because of my experience with the college administration. I'm willing to come in and discuss it and let you decide for yourself.

THEM: Well, we've already interviewed enough candidates and we have a couple who seem to be what we're looking for.

YOU: Fine. I can understand why you wouldn't want to interview anyone else. But I'd appreciate having the chance to meet with you briefly just so that we can both be sure we're not missing an opportunity.

TACTIC #58

List three objections which you feel will be raised during the course of your job campaign. Then write down one or two answers to each objection. When you are satisfied with these answers, role-play them with someone.

COMPLETION CHECK ☐

THE SECRETARIAL BLOCKADE

A large number of good job campaigns meet a temporary demise at a secretary's desk. This all-too-frequent interception mostly comes out of the unwillingness of the applicant to present her or his objective clearly to the secretary who gets on the line with one or both of the two classic stoppers:

"What's this in reference to?"

or

"Can I help you?"

These words can strike fear into the heart of an unprepared caller—but they can be handled, as you will see. Do *not* admit that you are in any way, shape, or form looking for a job, unless you are responding to an advertisement listing the name of the person you are calling. (For most of these strategies we assume that you are following the approach of creating your own job, out of your self-discovered personal targets.)

Keep in mind that the purpose of your call is not just to look for a job, but to talk to a particular person about a specific topic. So when the secretary says: "What's this in reference to?" instead of blurting out your real reason, simply say: "I want to talk with Mr. Webb about his new research project."

When she says: "Can I help you?" instead of saying "No" say "Yes, perhaps you can, I'm interested in knowing what kind of sampling techniques you will use," or some other technical point. Chances are you will be referred to her boss for the answer. If she does know the answer, thank her, and then ask if you can talk to Mr. Webb about it, and if this isn't a convenient time, what would be?

Probably the most effective way to get through is to sound as though you *should* be talking to Mr. Webb. In other words, sound reasonably assured and confident. After practicing calls to "important" people you will soon find that your tone of voice will get you through much of the time. Other techniques are:

- Call just before or after normal office hours. Sometimes the boss is in earlier or later than the secretarial help.
- Ask the organization's switchboard for the direct dial number rather than the person's name.
- Call the president's office, and ask, "Who would I talk to about —— ?" Use this referral to get you past the secretary. When she or he asks why you are calling, say Mr. (the president's name)'s office said you should. This implied referral will work most of the time.
- Try, try again. Don't leave your name and number, say that you plan to be out and will call back. This keeps the initiative on your side.

KEEP ON TRUCKING

The way you get interviews is to keep communicating value to the right people until they start to get it. There are two successful patterns to follow which use the phone call in connection with the cover letter and résumé. The most recommended is this:

1. Collect the names and phone numbers of 25 firms that you know could hire or have hired someone in a position which equates to or is close to one of your job targets.

2. Identify who the hiring authority is.

3. Call him until you get through.

4. Communicate a clear value and ask for a meeting. Listen to any objection and answer with a benefit. Ask again for the interview.

5. If the answer is yes, take your résumé with you to the interview.

6. If the answer is still no, after you have met at least one objection (you can go for more if you're up to it), ask the employer if you can send him a résumé. Most will say yes to this. If no, go on to the next firm.

7. If yes, prepare a well-thought-out cover letter and send it with a résumé.

8. Five days after you have sent it, call again to verify if he has received it. Quietly repeat the benefit and ask again for a meeting.

THE WAY IN

The other procedure we recommend omits the initial call. You begin with mailing the résumé and cover letter and do the follow-up call as a first call.

Q. Hold on. I'll get the phone slammed down in my face if I do all this calling. Why would anyone hire someone who can't understand the meaning of the word "no"?

A. Have you tried it?

Q. No, and I doubt that I will. It might work in New York, but not in the rest of the country.

A. How do you know?

Q. Well, if he liked what I have to say, he wouldn't say no.

A. That's not true. People frequently say no at first to almost any new idea. Ask any salesman. They are masters at hearing no. And they know that their job is to change the no to a yes. You must know that.

Q. Yes, but that's different. They're selling a product, not themselves.

A. They are selling neither. They're selling a benefit and they are communicating through a wall of doubts and skepticism.

Q. But how do you know it's a wall? They might not really need me.

A. The approach which we are recommending deals with the projection of value and benefit. The alternative seems to be to dramatize your needs. Which would you rather do?

Q. I don't know, I'm still afraid. I was never taught to project my value, only my liabilities. I could project a better image, I guess.

A. Exactly.

TACTIC #59

Establish a definite written schedule for phoning. Allocate specific dates and times in advance, and the number of calls you plan to complete on each date; then keep to your schedule. Acknowledge yourself when you meet your schedule and note if you do not. If you are consistently missing your schedule, adjust it downward to a level where you can experience making it.

COMPLETION CHECK ☐

DROP IN

It is possible to go into an office building in the center of a busy downtown area, look at the directory of tenants, write down the names of a dozen of them, stop by and get brochures, go to the coffee shop and read them, return and ask for an interview with a particular person, present your abilities, and get a job offer before lunch. We've seen it done. You might even want to try it. It's a little like doing a dozen laps in the swimming pool with your tennis shoes on. It builds muscle. And it can be a rewarding, expanding experience.

INFORMATION INTERVIEWS

It is easier to get interviews for the purpose of obtaining information than for selling yourself. So go after interviews with people in the field who wouldn't mind telling you how things work. Before the interview, prepare a list of questions you need answered. Be flattering but not cloying. By building up contacts through an information network, you set yourself up with good contacts and referrals. It is a good interview-getting technique.

THE AGENCY GAME

There are over ten thousand private, profit-making placement agencies interested in helping you get a new job. Most of them have a uniquely fair system for charging for their services. If they don't get you placed on a job, there is no fee. In many cases, even when you are placed on a job through the placement agency's efforts, the fee is paid to the agency by the hiring employer.

So what can you lose? If you do not conduct your relations with employment agencies with the same degree of conscious intention as the rest of your job campaign, you can lose time, direction, and the exciting personal satisfaction which can come when you are indeed in charge of your own career destiny.

If you manage it properly, however, you can establish a relationship with placement agencies which expands the dimensions of your self-directed career search. Here's how:

1. *Don't relinquish the responsibility and energy of your job search to a third party.* The employment counselor will often encourage you to leave matters in her or his hands. You'll be tempted, but don't. Apply the same standards of relationship to career goals and targets with the leads turned up by the agency as you would for your self-developed job prospects.

2. *Use placement agencies as part of your support system.* To do this, you must identify the areas where they can be most helpful to you. For example, they can usually offer you knowledge of local market conditions, ability to make employer contacts, knowledge of current salary offerings in particular areas, feedback on your résumé, and knowledge of specific employers.

3. *Make certain that the employment agent is clear about your self-developed job targets.* Don't allow a counselor (who may have an immediae job interview to send you out on) to convince you that you would be better off by changing your target to something more readily available. The temptation can be very strong. Resist it in favor of your own satisfaction-centered

targets. If the agency can't, or won't, support you in *your* goals, find another agency.

4. *Work with the best.* If you feel upon initial contact that an agency, or counselor, is not providing the top-quality support which you expect, tell them. If they don't improve to your standards, find someone who will.

5. *Support the agency that supports you.* Don't dump your job-finding problem in the agency's lap and walk away. Find out what you can do to make their job easier and better. Provide the counselor with copies of a good, well-printed résumé. Provide a list of potential employers from your research. Develop a clear statement of your unique selling propositions, the things you offer potential employers that create a clear, irresistible value, and give a copy of it to the counselor.

6. *Keep your agreements.* Stay in communication with the agency and counselor and show up at the interviews you agree to take. Call back and report when you have a change in status or direction. Acknowledge to the counselor the things that he or she has accomplished for you. With acknowledgment and thanks you can create miracles of motivation.

TACTIC #60

Use some imaginative research techniques to uncover the best personnel agency to work with you in your search. Do this by calling the personnel departments of several employers in fields related to your job targets and asking them for the names of agencies they work with. Then ask for the names of specific counselors at these agencies.

Call the agencies and counselors and tell them that you were recommended to them by the organizations from which you got their names. This implied referral can get you meetings with the best agency people in your field.

COMPLETION CHECK ☐

THE EXECUTIVE SUITE

Executive search firms specialize in the identification and placement of top-level personnel in salary ranges generally exceeding $25,000 per year. They charge large fees for their services to the employers who retain them. Executive search firms are not usually considered part of the normal marketplace. They do not provide the depth of job orders or referral information which might be available at an upper echelon employment agency.

The search firm customarily handles each new assignment separately. Through investigative recruitment techniques, which are not unlike those for locating employers described in this book, but are used to locate applicants, they go after people who are already well employed and entice them to consider new, and presumably better, opportunities with their client employer.

It is clear that the search firm's client is the employer, and that the employers who are signed up for searches at any particular moment in time are looking for very highly specialized talent. Search firms usually report to the board of directors of a firm, the president, or vice-president. They don't generally work with the personnel department.

You probably won't get specific job referrals from an executive search firm unless you are in a special high-growth area or have impeccable qualifications. However, a relationship with the specific purpose of assisting you put your job search in perspective can be valuable, since many of the search consultants are quite knowledgeable in specific fields.

If you are qualified in a high-level professional area, you can possibly establish a conversational relationship with an executive search firm in a way similar to the technique we discussed above on the identification of placement agencies.

Contact an executive with a firm in a field similar to your own job target. Tell the executive, or the executive's secretary, that you are interested in getting the name of a search firm and the name of one of the principal search consultants working with the firm. With the names of three or four search firm executives available to you, it should not be too difficult to arrange a meeting where you can pick the brains of an expert in the field of your job targets. This meeting will occur because of your ability to use the implied referral technique, a bit of flattering, and the search firms' natural tendency to want to meet people who are up and coming in their field.

If you set up such a meeting, go into it with a list of specific questions which someone at this level can help answer for you. You may find it hard to get the names of particular employers; however, indirect referral to reference sources and good knowledge of which firms are expanding and which are cutting back can speed up your work search.

EXECUTIVE COUNSELING

Are the services of a placement counseling firm worth $1500 to $3500 to assist you with your job campaign?

We don't know. We've heard from people who have experienced a successful working relationship with career counseling organizations and we have heard from people who have been ripped off by big promises, small delivery.

An executive counseling firm specializes in assisting job seekers, particularly those who are having difficulty in their job search campaigns, to implement a self-marketing program to employers whose names are provided by the counseling firm. The services are provided for a flat negotiated fee, which usually is payable whether you get a new job or not. The services provided vary considerably from firm to firm and from client to client. They can include testing, career planning, résumé and cover letter preparation, identification of employer prospects, and mailings. All this can provide a most valuable support to your job campaign if you have been unable to mobilize these activities on your own, but for the average worker it is an expensive substitute for his or her own organized campaign. If you have experienced difficulty getting your job search together, and feel that the organized push of a career counseling service is worth the cost, take the following steps before deciding:

1. Contact two or three separate firms. Compare services, cost, professionalism.

2. Ask to meet the people you would be working with in your campaign. They may not resemble the salesperson who signs you up.

3. Find out *specifically* what you will get for your money. If, for example, they promise an employer mailing, find out how large it will be, and where the names have come from. If the counseling firm plans to redo your résumé, ask to see others they have done.

4. Once you have gotten a clear description of what the firm plans to do for you, ask for it in writing.

5. If the counseling firm boasts of good contacts with employers in your field, ask for the names of some of the firms they have worked with recently and contact one or two employers at random to verify.

6. If you have any suspicion that the career counseling firm is promising more than it will or can deliver, check with your local Better Business Bureau to see if it has received any complaints.

7. Negotiate. It is frequently possible to get the same services for a reduced fee if you are reasonably tough, or eliminate parts of the program that are less valuable to you. Also, see if you can pay in installments, with an agreement that if you change your mind partway through the program you will not be obliged to pay the balance.

8. Do not give up your own responsibility in the matter of your job campaign just because you have engaged someone to assist you. Cooperate fully with the counselor you are working with, assist with whatever supportive research you can do, communicate whatever barriers or problems you face, and do your homework.

COLLEGE PLACEMENT OFFICES

Schools are becoming increasingly aware of, and involved in, the process by which their students make the transition from academic life to the pragmatic world of work, although most programs remain at a level which is, in our opinion, far below what is called for.

Many schools have split the responsibilities for career planning and placement into two departments: *counseling*, which is primarily involved with testing and measuring aptitudes and values, and assisting with vocational and academic choices; and *placement*, which is responsible for the actual job-match process—scheduling interviews on campus, providing referrals to full-time and part-time jobs, and maintaining career information facilities. The trend now is to combine these services into one career planning and placement department.

There are many career planning and placement offices that are very good: the placement and counseling functions working closely together to support the student in identifying and obtaining work situations which have at their base the individual's personal satisfaction and growth. At worst the two functions operate competitively, doing a poor job of expanding the student's understanding of his real work potential and concentrating primarily on the "placement rate," that is, how many students get jobs of any kind. This narrow view of the placement function can make the school look good—"95% of our students get jobs upon graduation" —and leave the student with a very narrow range of choice for the important entry into his worklife: "I interviewed three companies, got one offer, and the school recommended that I take it."

Many schools will allow people from the community to get assistance from the facilities of the career planning and placement departments in establishing job targets and even occasionally learning about specific job listings. So, even if you are not a college graduate or if you went to college elsewhere, check out the career planning and placement departments of the schools in your area.

THE WAY IN

Here are some of the resources you may be able to avail yourself of.

- Vocational and aptitude testing
- Qualified guidance and placement counselors
- Access to immediate available job listings
- Information about firms which are recruiting for specific fields
- Reference materials on specific career fields (books, trade journals, etc.)
- Employer materials—many schools maintain extensive libraries of employer information, such as annual reports, product information, and position descriptions
- Business directories
- Career guidance materials—books about the job search, sample résumés, etc.
- Lectures, workshops, career fairs.

TACTIC #61

Consult the Yellow Pages, the public library, or someone very familiar with the community colleges and four-year universities and colleges in your area. Through some investigatory phone calls, determine the names of the placement directors at these schools.

Next, find out what kind of community involvement the school has had in the past. Call the school president's office, find out from his secretary or assistant the name of the person at the school in charge of community relations and programs. Contact him to find out if the facilities of the placement/counseling center are ever made available to selected individuals from the community. (Don't scare her or him into thinking that by helping you it will open a floodgate.) If you get a green light, contact the placement director, give your referral, and lay out what it is you want to accomplish. If the community affairs director is not encouraging, thank her or him for the time spent and contact the placement director directly. Organize your approach to create the minimum of disruption and the maximum of acknowledgment and thanks for the value you have received (including a thank-you letter to the president of the school).

Try several schools until you have established a supportive relationship with one.

If you are a college graduate living in an area away from your old school, you can do the same thing without necessarily going through the community affairs tactic. You may want to contact the placement director of your own school and ask him to contact the local school to arrange for you to use their facilities. Or else just show up and ask for an appointment.

COMPLETION CHECK

STATE EMPLOYMENT SERVICE

Your local state employment service office can assist in your job search if you are seeking employment in an entry level, industrial, skilled or unskilled trade or craft position. In some cases, depending upon the local office, they may handle professional and white-collar jobs. The state employment service office will also have information about a variety of government-sponsored skill-training and counseling programs.

The employment service is another resource you can tap to support you in your work goals. It will not invest much time in assisting you to identify positions which support your life goals and personal aliveness. That is not its function. It is essentially a large-volume clearinghouse of lower-level jobs and supportive training and counseling activities.

If you are unemployed or looking for some needed upgrading of your skills, pay a visit to your local state employment service and ask for brochures describing the variety of services which they provide. Pick out the specific programs which appear to be most valuable and then, having armed yourself with the details, visit the office and meet a counselor to learn how the service applies to you and how you can employ it.

In your relation with the employment service, don't lose sight of the fact that *you* are responsible for getting the kind of job which works for you. The government won't do it for you.

GUERRILLA TACTICS IN THE JOB MARKET
REMINDERS AND REFERENCES

Reminders

- Communicate past accomplishments; not merely duties.
- Remember: résumés don't get jobs. The most they can do is get interviews.

References

The Perfect Résumé by Tom Jackson. Comtrain Inc., 300 Central Park West, New York, N.Y. 10024.

Management: Tasks, Responsibilities, Practices by Peter Drucker. Harper & Row, New York, 1974.

On Writing Well by William Zinsser. Harper & Row, New York, 1976.

For Women (from point of view of upward mobility): *The Managerial Woman* by Margaret Hennig and Anne Jardim. Anchor Press, Doubleday, New York, 1977.

Other Resources

For a list of executive search firms, write:
American Management Association
135 W. 50th St.
New York, N.Y. 10019

For a list of employment agencies, write:
National Employment Association
2000 K Street N.W.
Washington, D.C. 20006

Question: Are you completing the tactics that we provided throughout the book? They represent solid, proven ways for getting what you want.

9

THE
DIRECTED
INTERVIEW

FRESH START

Everything you have done so far in your job search has led to this moment of truth in the employment process—the meeting between you and your potential employer. Regardless of how sloppy your job campaign has been up to this time, or how long it has taken, and despite the fact that you may not be satisfied with your résumé, or that you may not have done as well as you would have liked in previous interviews, the next interview you have rolls the scoreboard back to zero.

The employment interview is something like a courtship in which the parties are interested in each other, but wary of hidden flaws, uncommunicated concerns, or questionable past history. Everything is possible. Or nothing.

We asked our employer panel for their suggestions of ways applicants could improve their performances in the interview. Here's what they said:

> Employer No. 1: "They need to know more about us and to be able to converse easily about the basics of our business. They don't need a detailed history, but they need to know something about our products and our goals."
>
> Employer No. 2: "An applicant should come to the interview ready to tell me what she or he can do for us. If she is a secretary, I want to hear how she can organize and get out the workload. If she is a salesperson, I want her to know our product. I get tired of hearing only what the applicant *wants* from the job."
>
> Employer No. 3: "One very important factor in a person's physical presentation is how the person is dressed, the way he or she holds himself. Neatness. You'd be surprised how many good applicants get turned down because of a sloppy appearance."

Employer No. 2: "Another thing. The candidate should be willing to ask questions, to let us know what his or her standards are, and what he or she wants to know about us. It doesn't make a good impression for an applicant to just sit there and wait for me to decide what to ask."

Employer No. 3: "I agree. Many applicants are so nervous that they come across far more timid than they really are. It's OK to be a little assertive in the interview. I think it would help if people would practice before they went out for interviews. It would loosen them up."

Employer No. 4: "I think that what we've all been saying is that an interview is a sales situation, and the applicant has to present himself or herself, as the product, in the best light."

TACTIC #62

If you have previously looked for work, think back over any interviews you have had, and list the ways you could have been more effective.

COMPLETION CHECK ☐

THE IRRESISTIBLE MESSAGE

Most job seekers envision the interview as a minor inquisition. They think the employer's purpose is to prove how bad they are in order to screen them out. Fear of rejection is frequently the overriding element in the candidate's approach. It is helpful to look at the meeting from the interviewer's point of view. One thing becomes clear rather quickly: The goal of the interviewer is not at all like the images in the candidate's fearful expectations. For one thing, *the interviewer is usually very interested in hiring someone for the job as soon as possible.* After all, the purpose of the organization is not to be in the employment game, but to get the job done. The sooner they identify and hire the right person the sooner they can get on with their real work.

Employers are not doing anyone a favor when they hire them. In the most basic terms they are making a purchasing decision: identifying a capability and capacity which will fit their needs, and then hiring the person who has it.

Employers profit by hiring. That's why they do it. The employer you are nervously waiting to see is probably just as nervously hoping you are going to be the one so he can give up interviewing and get back to work.

In most cases, the employer is waiting to hear a simple positive statement from the candidate which expresses clearly what the employer is looking for. The message is really not as involved and complex as most job seekers think. It is simply the answer to the generally inarticulated question: *"Why should I hire you?"* This is the underlying context of the interview for the employer which the candidate must satisfy before an offer can be made.

The problem is that most candidates don't really address themselves to this question at all. Most candidates are dramatizing an almost opposite communication: *"I need a job."* And so the interview frequently becomes a game in which the employer is forced to dig for the answers himself.

Another thing observed very frequently in videotaped interviews is the tendency for applicants to put out communications which almost thwart their objective of getting a job offer. It is surprisingly true. Even the way many candidates are dressed—in frayed shirts, poorly fitting or wrinkled suits or dresses, and inappropriate styles—communicates that they may not be the ones for the position.

Also observed is that frequent tendency to lead with negative information: "I haven't worked for a while, but I think I could do it," or "I don't know if I can handle it or not, but I'm willing to try." Such communications dramatize uncertainty and lack of confidence. Anger and resentment also show under the surface in a variety of conscious and unconscious ways, such as sullenness, lack of communication, low energy, and even caustic comments masquerading as superiority.

The message that is irresistible to an employer is the message that makes him feel confident of two things:

- Your ability to contribute to the solution of the problems he faces. Your skills or aptitude.
- Your willingness to do what's necessary to get the job done. In other words, your attitude.

It isn't necessary that you have a detailed advance technical knowledge of the specific operation or need of the employer; your willingness to get the work done will see to that. What is most important is that you demonstrate your underlying motivation. The fact that you have done any research at all indicates an attitude which is already attractive.

TACTIC #63

> If you are now working, list three activities or tasks which you perform which make a direct measurable contribution to your employer. Write them in terms of accomplishments rather than duties. If you are not working, think of an employer you know of and would like to work for, and list three ways you can contribute. After you have written these, communicate them verbally to someone in your support system.
>
> COMPLETION CHECK ☐

EMPLOYERS DON'T KNOW

There is no guarantee that the employer representative you meet will ask the right questions to enable you to present the information you want the representative to know. Often the employer representative (if outside of personnel) will know very little about good interviewing techniques. He or she may be a big socializer or spend the interview proving how terrific he or she is and what intelligent questions he or she can ask.

Your job in such a situation is *to direct the interview yourself.* Now, quickly, before you go running off to your next interview like an infantry recruit, let us explain what we mean. We don't mean that you dominate the interview, or bully the interviewer into listening to what you say. It does mean *that you will take full responsibility to ensure that the employer hears what you want him or her to know about you.*

You do this by remaining conscious throughout the meeting, by knowing in advance the specific things about yourself that you want the recruiter to know, and by being able to lightly steer the conversation in the directions you want it to go. This can be done without apparent effort by mastering a few simple communications techniques.

- Keep your eyes and attention on the interviewer. This will tend to keep the interviewer on course and minimize wanderings.
- Use directly related questions to bring the interview back on course, e.g., "Yes. That's interesting. Could you tell me how many orders a week are processed through this department?"
- Ask for the opportunity to communicate about yourself, e.g., "Would you be interested in hearing about my responsibilities regarding our weekly reports?"
- Ask for feedback with questions such as: "Do you think that what I've told you about myself fits what you are looking for? What other areas would you like to explore?"

As an adroit interviewee, you will direct the conversation along the paths which you feel are most supportive of your getting an offer.

PREPLAN

No professional pilot would think of taking off on an important flight without investing a reasonable amount of time in preplanning. The more thorough this planning is, the more comfortable and precise the flight will be.

The better you plan in advance for your interview,

THE DIRECTED INTERVIEW

the more comfortable you will be in it, and the more able you will be to communicate that you are a valuable prospect for the employer.

Good preparation for the interview provides you with several very real advantages:

- You will not have to waste valuable time finding out general information about the organization, which gives you extra time to present yourself.
- You will know in advance what aspects of yourself to emphasize to suit the employer's needs or objectives.
- You can prepare notes to consult during the interview to ensure against forgetting.
- With good preparation you will be more comfortable and therefore better able to listen and observe.
- By anticipating possible negative aspects of your background which will come up, you can prepare appropriate responses and avoid possible embarrassment.
- With advance preparation, you can focus the interview in directions which satisfy your personal job targets.
- By knowing in advance what salary range is contemplated, you can probably negotiate for more money than if you were unprepared.
- With even a moderate amount of advance planning you will make a substantially better impression than most other job seekers.

It is clear that you have a lot at stake: the research, the phone calls, the turndowns and turnoffs. Many hours of effort and activity can be spent obtaining each interview, so it makes sense to protect your investment with an additional hour or two of research and planning. Here are some of the most important things you can find out before the interview:

- What products or services does the employer produce or perform? Find out about all of them, not just the area of your interest.
- How are their products or services looked upon in their industry. What is their reputation?
- Who are their competitors? What are they doing in the same field? What new advances are being made?
- What are some of the common industry problems with government regulation, etc.?

- What are the most important tasks or problems facing the particular department or division in which you would work?
- List all the tasks you can think of which are probably associated with the job in one way or another. Then match each task with a related skill or ability of your own.
- What major organizational changes have taken place in the past few years? How have the effects been felt in your targeted department?
- What are some of the major activities which have occurred in the past year or six months?

Note: Depending on the level of your target job and other factors of competition, you may wish to research some of the items on the above list and skip others. But don't make the mistake of thinking that because you are after a clerical or secretarial job the items on the sheet are irrelevant to you. Nothing could be further from the truth. More than a few secretaries have gotten better, higher-paying jobs because they were able to demonstrate a knowledge of the organization to an employer.

Q. Enough is enough. You can't expect me to do all of this stuff for every interview.
A. Why not?
Q. Well, it's too much work, there just isn't enough time.
A. How many interviews do you have scheduled?
Q. Well there's one with Firemen's Mutual next week, and probably a couple after that.
A. When?
Q. I don't know.
A. So what's the big problem with time?
Q. Well it's not just the time, it's also that I don't believe it's necessary to do all this stuff. Why not just go in for the job like everyone else?
A. You can do that if you want your job campaign to look like everyone else's. On the other hand, you might want to go in with a competitive edge so you can have a better-than-average chance to get what you want.

THE DIRECTED INTERVIEW

- Q. It just looks phony and pretentious. Besides, they're going to decide whether to hire me or not based on whether I can do the job, not because I know how many offices they have or what the company president eats for breakfast.
- A. Funny. Do you agree that presenting yourself for a job is a sales situation?
- Q. Yes, although I don't like it. They should hire me based on how good I am, not how well I can sell myself.
- A. How will they know how good you are if you don't tell them?
- Q. OK, you win, it is a sales situation.
- A. Good. Now if it's a sales situation, don't you think you could do a better job of selling if you know what they are looking to buy?
- Q. Yes, it seems to make sense, but why have people been able to get along so long without doing all this?
- A. The people with the best jobs *have* been doing this. The people who have just taken the next job which comes along haven't. Are you willing to get the kind of job which would actually be what you want, and give you pleasure as well as a paycheck?
- Q. Yes, but it looks like work to do it, and I don't want to put in the time.
- A. I know. That's what the problem really is, you don't want to put in the time.
- Q. You're right. That's where I'm stuck.

TACTIC #64

Pick five employers you wish to interview, or have scheduled for interviews. Call or write each employer (or stop by if you are rushed for time) and obtain a copy of their annual report (if public), capabilities brochure, product information, and issues of the employer newsletter, if any. You can contact their advertising, public information, sales department. Do this before each interview.

COMPLETION CHECK ☐

ABOUT YOU

The outside research we've just outlined is an essential first step in your preplanning. Once that's done, you need to look inside and polish up those things about yourself which will make the best impression and make the interview go most smoothly for you.

The applicant who goes into an interview with little preparation very often finds when it's all over, that important things about himself or herself were left out and that the applicant was unprepared for some of the questions asked. Here are some of the ways you can best prepare yourself for interivews:

- Identify and write down specific problem-solving skills or experiences which you can demonstrate, and which would assist the organization to meet its needs.
- Get the names of two or three well-respected people who will vouch for your abilities.
- Anticipate any parts of your background or experience which may be seen as negative by the employer, and construct and write down an approach which has a chance of overcoming this negativism.
- Determine and write down the key personal goals you would expect to have satisfied in the job, so you can clearly evaluate whether or not you want it.
- Select some examples of your work which might be appropriate to bring with you to the interview.
- Research and determine a realistic and desired salary target, and be clear about the minimum offer you will consider.

TACTIC #65

Make a list of a number of questions you feel would be hardest for you to answer, things such as "Why have you been unemployed for five months?" or "Why were you terminated from your last job?" List the things you hope won't be asked.

Get a tape recorder, ask yourself each question, and answer it on the tape. Then play back the answer and critique it. Continue to do this until you are satisfied with how you have answered these questions.

COMPLETION CHECK ☐

DRESSING FOR SUCCESS

The way you dress is the single most important nonverbal communication you make about yourself.

Let that sink in. A surprising number of applicants, especially those just entering or reentering the job market, undermine their job campaign by the way they dress. A frequent attitude is: "If they don't like me the way I am, that's too bad," or "I'll be able to dress better *after* I get the job."

Please understand that to most people meeting you for the first time, the way you look is the way you are. That is where the interview *starts*. You may move up or down from that place, but probably not very far.

It is interesting to observe how people allow (or cause) their clothes to reflect the way they see themselves. A successful executive *looks* different from a person who is worried about his job. People who are experiencing a low self-image frequently dramatize that picture of themselves by dressing in sloppy, ill-fitting garments, inappropriate styles, frayed collars, poorly matched colors, run-down shoes, and so forth.

Part of your planning for the interview should be to put together clothes which will support you in making a good impression. Your clothes have only one purpose, to support you in getting what you want in life. In other words, decide what you *want* and dress for that, rather than just put on what you happen to own.

The best way to approach dressing is to identify people you feel have already become successful, notice how they are dressed, and do likewise. Some basic rules:

- For most organizations you should tend to dress on the conservative side. People in business don't like surprises. Set aside particular clothes you will wear for work. These will differ from your dress-up clothes and from the things you wear to knock about the house.
- Pick fabrics which will not show wrinkles. Synthetics and blends will do admirably, particularly those which have been textured to look like fine wools.
- Make sure your clothes fit you. Spend the extra money to have garments custom-fitted.
- Don't try to be too individualistic in your approach. You should not stand out dramatically from the people you will be working with, particularly at the interview stage. On the other hand, don't totally adopt a uniform. Add a bit of individual flair to good basics.
- Women moving from secretarial or household duties into management training should specifically reappraise their outfits, and move toward conservative suits, well-made skirts and blouses, and simple jewelry.
- Students wishing to move into management training and similar responsibilities may have to invest $200 to $300 for a good-looking business outfit. This should be done *before* the interviews.
- Avoid wearing clanking jewelry or heavy fragrances which will call attention to themselves.
- Male or female, for most office or professional jobs bring an attaché case or briefcase. This is the premier business accessory.

TACTIC #66

Use the buddy system to help organize your clothes before starting interviews. Have someone qualified by employment and experience be a friendly critic of how you look, giving you feedback on how your present wardrobe works for the level of interviews you want. Encourage him or her to be as frank as possible. Write down the things you need. Take your buddies shopping with you.

COMPLETION CHECK ☐

FIRST IMPRESSIONS LAST

For years we have been convinced that the first impression you make is an important determinant of the success or failure of an interview. Testing this out recently by analyzing videotaped employment interviews, we were surprised to find out that not only was the initial impression important, in many cases it virtually controlled the results of the interview.

We saw employer representatives appear to make up their minds within the first five or ten minutes and then, throughout the balance of the interview, ask questions which would produce answers to justify the decision already reached. Applicants would go right along with it. If the employer was positively inclined, the applicant would relax, smile, and play out the interview without half trying. If the employer had decided "no" in the opening minutes, and communicated it either through the type of question or nonverbally, the applicant would appear to accept the inevitable, literally slump in her or his chair, and lose interest.

This is not to say that a poor first impression will necessarily doom the interview. Using good techniques it is possible to turn the whole thing around. However, just as in a master chess game, or the Super Bowl, once you get behind, it is very hard to catch up.

Besides your personal appearance, there are things you should accomplish within the first five or ten minutes of the interview which will get the process off to a head start.

1. Establish rapport. Greet the interviewer with a welcoming smile, immediate eye contact, and high energy.

2. Acknowledge or compliment the interviewer for something about his organization that you have learned or observed, such as a new product or the appearance of the offices.

3. Establish communication. Show that you are attentive and interested, that you hear what the interviewer is saying. If the meeting is getting off to a slow start, ask a question or make a comment that shows your willingness to communicate about the job.

An important question to ask at the beginning of the interview is: "Could you tell me what it is you are looking for in the person who does this job?" Pay attention as the employer lays out what he or she is looking for and feed it back during the interview.

4. Demonstrate by your comments and questions that you are most interested in finding out how you can assist the employer in accomplishing the job. Answer questions from this point of view.

After ten minutes take stock of how your opening moves have worked. Is the employer representative interested in what you are saying? See if you have been able to communicate your accomplishments, or if it has been appropriate for you to ask questions. Observe your own speech patterns and check for posture and breathing. If you notice that you are tense, RELAX. Put in whatever correction is called for, and continue.

TACTIC #67

Before each interview, write down on one side of a 3 x 5 index card five of your accomplishments (results) that you want the employer to know about. On the other side of the card list five intelligent questions to ask the employer to assist you in determining whether you wish to work in this organization. (Save questions about vacation, benefits, salary, etc., until you have received an offer.)

COMPLETION CHECK

RECEIVING AND TRANSMITTING

As we said earlier, most people don't communicate very well. Generally when someone is telling you something, you are thinking about all of the things you want to say when the other party stops. And while you are talking, the other party is evaluating and judging what you are saying, and thinking up something to say in return. *There is very little listening or communicating going on in most conversations—and, of course, in most interviews.*

- Remember that real communication requires that you be 100% responsible that a message is received, either by you or the other party.
- If a question is asked which you don't understand, don't jump in with an answer; clarify the question first. If you don't know the answer, say so. There is no quicker way to disqualify yourself than by making things up.
- Keep observing the interviewer to see if what you are saying is getting through. If not, turn up the intensity of your intentions.
- Avoid superfluous information. Answer the question with the required information, add anything which you feel to be appropriate, and then stop talking or ask a relevant question.

- Look for nonverbal signals. Don't try to figure them out exactly, but if you see the employer's attention wandering (finger tapping, eyes glazed over), change the subject or ask a question.
- Answer questions, not statements, If the employer comments about your background or experience, acknowledge the statement, and avoid adding information unless it is clearly called for, or in your best interest.
- Keep coming back to the main subject. This is what you can do to support the purpose of the organization and/or the position. Communicate that clearly at every moment.
- Get feedback. Don't allow the interview to play itself out without knowing how you are coming across. Stop and ask: "Do you feel that this is the kind of experience which could be valuable to your firm? Or ask a similar question whose answer will show you what you have accomplished.
- Lighten up. Don't be so serious that the interview is without humor. Remember they want to hire someone who will be pleasant to work with. Smile, laugh, be amused as frequently as you can and still be appropriate.
- Correct. If you are midway into the interview and sense that you are not doing as well as you could, don't write off the balance of the meeting. Correct the situation immediately by getting your energy up—moving into other areas, or getting back on track.

TACTIC #68

In the interview, demonstrate to the employer what you can do for him. Put together some samples of your work, or anything else which you can leave behind or show the interviewer during the meeting. Remember, "a picture is worth a thousand words."

COMPLETION CHECK

INFORMATION EXCHANGE

There are three main areas where the employer looks for information on which to base a hiring decision:

Education and training
Work experience
Personality factors

In the interview he is primarily guided by his own, generally rather inexact, idea of what the job entails. If the interviewer is within the personnel function and interviewing in response to an advertised position, you will probably find that he is rather strictly interpreting some very specific criteria for type and duration of experience, education level attained, and other qualifications. Since he has received this information from someone else, and it may not be a subject area in which he has direct experience, he will frequently not exercise much flexibility.

When you have an interview with someone who is in a position to make a hiring decision, you will find much more flexibility in getting to the basic question of your value to the organzation. This is particularly true when you have approached the employer through your own creative job market research. The closer the person is to the actual problem being discussed, the easier it is to talk in terms of solution and benefit rather than education and experience.

A typical interview may start with an open-ended question such as "Tell me about your work experience," which allows you the flexibility of presenting yourself in more or less your own terms, and then narrow down to closed-ended questions such as "Have you operated a mag card typewriter?" Then there might be a probe question challenging something you said: "How sure are you that you could supervise that many workers?" This cycle is repeated to cover the three major information categories listed above.

THE TELEGRAPH

Very often interviewers will clearly show what they are looking for by the way they ask questions. "You wouldn't mind doing some traveling, would you?" is a sample of a question that "telegraphs" the answer. There are many such questions, and if you keep your listening apparatus tuned in you will pick up many clues to what traits are being sought.

Of course, the best interviewers give the least information, leaving the responsibility more in your hands. Keep looking for things to communicate which demonstrate your ability to produce results. Use picture words. Read what the personnel director of one of the nation's largest firms looks for:

> I think that the key word for what we are looking for is mastery. We learned a long time ago that past experience is not a guarantee of future performance. The fact that a person has five years experience doing one thing doesn't mean that they are going to be able to do what the new position calls for. It's that old question—did the person have five years of active experience, or one year of experience five times over? I look for the way a person has handled all the things they are involved in and whether they mastered them.
>
> Take a college student, not much opportunity to gain experience in the particular fields we are involved in, but certainly enough lifetime to demonstrate an ability to master whatever he's been involved in. It's this ability to accomplish results that we want. Who knows what problems we are going to face in our business tomorrow; past experience won't help. We apply this as much as we can across the board from clerical on up. It may not be the traditional way to evaluate applicants, but it's the direction that many organizations are starting to move toward.

TACTIC #69

At the beginning of each interview (particularly interviews based upon unadvertised jobs), after the formalities, ask the recruiter this question: "Could you tell me in your own words what you are looking for in this position?" and then listen. Most recruiters will give you a description of what they are looking for. Pay attention, take mental notes. For the balance of the interview feed back to the recruiter the things he has said he is looking for.

COMPLETION CHECK ☐

HANDLING NEGATIVES

Frequently what controls applicants in an interview are the things about themselves which they see as negative. This preoccupation with past failures or shortcomings often plays itself out with the candidate ashamedly blurting out the horrible truth: that he or she got fired from his past job, or took off six months and went to Europe, or has only secretarial experience and now wishes to move to supervisory or management work. Here are a few rules for dealing with things you feel to be negative:

Rule 1. *Things are generally only negative in context*—that is, in the way that you treat them. It is your thoughts about activities which communicate the negative energy. If you apologize and look guilty about your six-month vacation from work, the interviewer will understand for sure that you did something you shouldn't have. If on the other hand you are proud of it and the life experience it gave you, the recruiter will look upon it as an asset. Even having been fired can be communicated as a positive learning experience.

Rule 2. *Don't dwell on negatives.* Simply admit them and move on. Don't apologize or overexplain. Everyone has some shortcomings or mistakes.

Rule 3. *Balance negatives with positives.* If it is noted that you have been out of work for six months, acknowledge this and move on to describe how able you now are to solve the employer's problems. A strong positive can erase the experience of a preceding negative.

TACTIC #70

List three things about yourself which you feel will appear as negatives. Underneath each one, list an offsetting positive characteristic.

COMPLETION CHECK [ ]

SAMPLE QUESTIONS

Shown below are five questions which summarize most of what you will be asked in interviews. If you can handle these five questions clearly and well and communicate mastery and accomplishment at the same time, you are well on your way to effective interviewing.

1. What are your strongest abilities?
2. How do your skills relate to our needs?
3. What are you looking for in a job?
4. What would you like to know about us?
5. Why should we hire you?

TACTIC #71

Get someone to role-play with you or use a tape recorder and answer the above five questions out loud, followed by an honest critique. Keep at it until the results are perfect.

COMPLETION CHECK [ ]

QUESTION-ABLE BEHAVIOR

Do ask questions. Ask clear, unambiguous questions about the firm you are interviewing. Ask what their objectives are. Where are they going to be in five years? What do they feel they offer a person?

Ask technical questions if you can: words per minute, cost per thousand, passengers per seat mile. Demonstrate through your questions that you know the subject and are *already* looking for solutions.

Don't be afraid to discuss touchy areas: pollution, profits, prices, hiring policies. Just don't put the employer down. Keep coming from supporting the employer, and offering solutions to his problems.

Do not ask about benefits, vacation, holidays, pensions, and working hours until you know you have an offer.

IS THE PRICE RIGHT?

It is essential that you make a conscious effort to keep your earnings high and rising, and that you follow a specific career development plan which is designed to maintain and expand your earnings through promotions, raises, and job changes.

You already know that the primary theme of this book is for you to use the years of your worklife as an opportunity to create satisfaction for yourself and value for others. We do not encourage people to take jobs which offer little personal reward beyond the paycheck. On the other hand, we know that it is definitely possible to combine good earnings with fulfilling, rewarding work.

Don't use the fact that you love the work as an excuse to shortchange your paycheck. Many highly skilled and productive workers, by assuming a passive role regarding their salary, end up making thousands of dollars less each year than others with similar abilities and interests.

Outside of union-protected work and highly bureaucratic jobs, *salary advancement does not happen automatically.* Like other areas of your career growth, it will flourish and expand if you take responsibility for it, and it won't if you don't. Without an assertive salary program you can find yourself down several thousand dollars a year, with very little chance of catching up. One of the dynamics at work in the job game is that after you have been working for a few years people tend to evaluate your abilities based upon how much money you are making in relation to others in the same field. In other words, despite the fact that you are excellent in your chosen field, if you don't keep your earnings on the high side of the range, you will be seen to be less capable than others who make more. So even if you aren't that interested in the extra money, go after it anyway to increase your power and effectiveness in the field. Here are some of the basic salary negotiation techniques to use in job changing and on the job:

- Always have a target figure in mind for right now and for one year from now. Stay in touch with the earnings of others in the field, watch employment ads in several cities, and get salary information from a trade or professional organization.
- As a candidate for a new job find out what the salary is *before* you go for the interview if you can. Do what you can to have the employer name a salary figure first. If you are in effect creating a new job, you can pose a question such as: "What do you feel that a position like this would be worth?"
- If the employer states a salary range that is satisfactory, always verbalize the top of the range. He says: "The range for the job is twelve to fourteen thousand per year." You say: "Fourteen thousand would be fine."
- Never answer the question "What is the minimum salary you would accept?" with an amount. Respond with: "I don't have a figure in mind, but I am looking at several possible situations, and will accept the one

which offers the best combination of opportunity and salary."
- Never accept an offer when it is given. Instead, respond with something like: "Thank you for the offer, I appreciate your confidence and know that I could make a contribution. Let me think about it for a few days and get back to you. I want to make sure that I make the right choice."
- Always go for a 10% increase over what you are offered. This is a tough one, particularly if you are anxious to get an attractive position, but, if properly followed, it can be worth many thousands of dollars over your career.

  Simply call back a day or two after the offer was made, communicate again how you feel you can make a strong contribution, and then suggest that the salary offered is shy of what you were looking for by an amount double the 10% increase you seek. Ask the employer to increase his offer and to split the difference (your 10% objective). Don't capitulate immediately if the employer doesn't come up with the extra money. The most successful negotiations are those in which a party is willing to stick with a fair demand.
- The cardinal role in all salary negotiations is that *money follows value.* If you want more money create more value, even if you don't immediately get paid for it. By continuing to feed value into the system, you will build up your worth, both to the organization and to yourself. After you have established your valuable contribution, you are in position to go for an increase to bring your compensation up to your value. Don't make the mistake that so many make of going after an increase on the grounds that you "need more money" and then, if you don't get it, lessening the quality of your performance. If you are not able to increase your compensation as you increase your value to the employer, and if you have communicated this responsibly, start to look for another game to play. Do this, not out of a sense of disloyalty to your employer, but out of loyalty to yourself.

TACTIC #72

Write down how much money you should, or would like to, be making five years from now. Working backward, list target figures for each year from the target year to now, that is, what you are now making or the figure you should go after now. Do whatever research is necessary to confirm the validity of the figures for the particular job target area. If the prevailing salaries within a given field do not meet your salary expectations, see how you can adjust your job target within your range of satisfaction and aliveness.

After you have determined your targets, ask yourself this question: What do I need to do to obtain these targets? Write down the answers.

COMPLETION CHECK ☐

ROLE PLAYING

Going into an interview without some form of rehearsal or role playing is like giving a speech without practicing. The speech may be good, but it won't be the best you can do. The purpose of role playing is to give you an opportunity to put theory into practice and to get valuable feedback in a simulated interviewing situation. The difficulty is that it takes time and organization to set it up and a willingness to encourage criticism.

You can participate in role plays at several levels, from practicing answers to only the difficult questions, or the five sample questions suggested above, or by doing a complete interview.

The most effective role-playing situations involve four people, at least one of whom has had experience as an interviewer or personnel consultant.

Here is how to set up interviewing role plays:

1. Set up a time and place in advance for yourself and two or three others. Allow the others to prepare so they can participate as candidates as well if they wish (good practice even if they are not in the job market).

THE DIRECTED INTERVIEW

2. If you haven't done so, prepare a résumé and have at least four copies of it.

3. Write out a brief description of a job opening on top of a sheet of paper. At the bottom, list some questions which you feel are difficult to answer. Make three copies.

4. When you assemble the group, arrange the chairs as though around a small square table, but without a table there, so that the applicant (you) is *directly* across from the person playing the employer, and the other two (observers) are on either side of the grouping.

5. Give each of the other three a copy of the résumé and job listing, and allow five minutes for them to read it. Suggest that the person taking the first turn as the employer start to think of questions he wishes to ask in addition to the ones you have provided.

6. Have the observers put their papers down and instruct them that their job is to observe closely, remaining silent, with the objective of coming up with suggestions of how you can improve your interviewing technique.

7. When everyone is clear about the instructions, begin the interview. Plan for a ten-minute interview (one of the observers should be timekeeper).

8. During the practice interview stay in your role. Resist the temptation to make comments. Present yourself as you would if it were a real interview.

9. At the end of the interview, the observers and the person who played the employer representative should feed back to you all the ways you could have improved your presentation. While this critique is going on you should be careful *not* to explain or apologize or even comment on the criticism, except to acknowledge and encourage it. This is very important, because people generally resist what appears as criticism. In this process it is a must.

10. After you have completed one cycle you may change employers and redo the same interview, or change players or job targets as you wish.

TACTIC #73

Select two or three other people to spend an hour with you in role plays. Set up a time and place, and carry out the preceding instructions.

COMPLETION CHECK

THE WRAP-UP

Don't leave any interview without knowing clearly where you stand with the employer. As you near the end of the meeting you should get some feedback on how you have come across, and what, if any, additional information may be required. Do this by directly asking a question such as "Do you feel that you have enough information?" or "Is there any area where you need more information?" or even more directly, "Do you feel that I have the basic qualifications you are looking for?"

Depending upon the answers you get from these questions, you will continue the determination of where you stand, or possibly put in some "correction" regarding areas where it is clear that the employer needs more information or support to produce a positive answer. Don't leave out this final push. Even if you are not certain whether you would accept an offer, it is a good policy to get as many offers as you can. It's good for your confidence.

If things are proceeding on a positive note, your move is now to ask, "What's the next step? Is there someone else in the organization I should see?" or a similar question designed to keep things moving along. Try to push for clarity at this point. Make it apparent without being pushy that you have other situations which are pending and you would like to do whatever you can to move things along.

The communication that *you do not need the employer* is one of the most valuable that you can accomplish.

Through this communication you suddenly become more valuable, less anxious to "get a job" and apparently more sought after.

Don't go off the deep end and start to lay down demands. Do disconnect your survival drive and ask for the kind of directness and communication which you'd expect from an alert organization. And make sure they know they are getting a good deal if they get you.

In the next chapter we'll show you how to capitalize on some of the seeds you've just planted.

REMINDERS AND REFERENCES

Reminders

- The way you dress is the most important nonverbal communication. A wrinkled suit/skirt implies a wrinkled mind.
- Remember: communicate value and benefits to an employer, *not need*. The essential question in every interview is "Why should I hire you?"
- The way to make more money is to produce more value.

References

Contact: The First Four Minutes by Leonard & Natalie Zunin. Ballantine, New York, 1975.

The Interviewer's Manual by Henry Morgan and John Cogger. The Psychological Corporation, Harcourt Brace Jovanovich, New York, 1973.

28 Days to a Better Job by Tom Jackson. Hawthorn Books, New York, 1977.

10

END GAME

OUT OF SIGHT, OUT OF MIND

Don't stop now. The game goes on and it is possible to score valuable points in the last moments of play. It is also possible to lose the game.

Most people get to the interview stage of their job campaign, do a pretty good job of communicating to the potential employers, and then sit back and wait for the job offers to start coming in. And they are frequently disappointed. Why is it that the big one, where they really had the great interview, hasn't responded?

Richard Blue

It's the job jitters again for Rich Blue, who has had six interviews and is waiting for a response. As he waits, he slowly builds up resentment and frustration. "Mr. Nelson said he would get back to me shortly. It's been three weeks. What do I do?"

Meanwhile, in his hectic Fresno office, John Nelson, city manager, is buried in six weeks' worth of paperwork. The 600-page evaluation of last year's shortage sits on his desk like a monument to his frustration. The budget for the City College is half done, correspondence is unanswered, a dozen phone calls are unreturned.

Despite 12-hour days and Saturday work, the backlog appears to expand rather than diminish. Nelson replays in his head one more time the decision to terminate Alex Bosch. Perhaps if he had known how difficult it was going to be to get a replacement . . . but, no, it was the right move. Alex was clearly creating more problems than he was solving. He'd been wrong for the job in the first place, but how can you tell in a short interview? Oh, interviews. With a weary sigh, Nelson recalls the folder of résumés on his desk. To top everything, no assistant and not even enough time to hire one.

"I've seen six candidates," he muses, "out of 50

résumés that are in the ball park. How many more people should I see? Ten? I can't even remember much about the six I've already seen. There was one woman that stood out, Kathy I think it was, I can remember her clearly. But she seemed shy. I don't know if she could handle the public appearances. And the other good one, what was his name? Green? Blue, that's it, Richard Blue. It's already been a couple of weeks. I liked him, but there was something not clear about the interview. What was it? If only I had taken better notes. I remember that I was going to get back to him and that I liked him, but there was something missing. I think I was concerned because he hadn't had enough government experience. I guess I'd better get some more interviews set up soon. Maybe one of them will have the perfect combination."

The phone rings and his secretary tells him Mr. Rich Blue is calling from Modesto. "He probably wants to find out what I decided. What do I say? I did promise to get back to him. I'll pretend I'm in a meeting. Oh hell, I'll talk to him."

"Hello, Blue, this is Nelson, thanks for calling. Look, I'm sorry that I haven't gotten back to you sooner. It's just that I . . ."

"Oh, listen, Mr. Nelson, don't worry about that. I could tell how busy you were just by looking at your desk. How are you coming with your budget?"

"Don't remind me! I think maybe I've read six pages of it since I last saw you."

"Seems to me that you could use that new assistant pretty soon." Blue laughs. "By the way, Mr. Nelson, do you remember telling me how you felt your budgeting procedures were significantly different from those we use in industry?"

"Yes, frankly, I've got to tell you that still bothers me. I don't know if we could take the time to train you in the system that we use. That's one of the things we've been thinking about." Nelson feels relieved that he can talk about the problem so easily.

Blue replies, knowing that his follow-up plan is working, "Yes, I knew you were concerned, so I decided to look into it. I spent a day at the Modesto

City Hall looking through their budgeting procedures and the actual budgets for the last two years."

Nelson is really tuning in now. Blue goes on with his planned follow-up: "I can tell you, Mr. Nelson, that you don't have to worry about a thing in that area. The procedures are almost identical to the approach we used to follow in the army six years ago, when I was the finance officer at Travis. Give me a couple of days and we'll have the whole thing handled."

Nelson's eyes stray to the budget folder on his desk. He thinks to himself, "Maybe I ought to decide on someone now and get this office back in shape. I'll never find the perfect person."

Blue continues his presentation, "One more thing, Mr. Nelson, as I went through that budget, I had some ideas about how we could possibly computerize the major points. You know, that's one of the things I did in this past job."

Blue feels a wave of relief move over him. This one has what he is looking for. "That might be more costly than we could handle right now. It's a good idea, and we've talked about it before, but until this water situation clears up we've got to hold back on the costs."

"Yes, I know. But I have an idea that we could use some existing commercial programs which are available for very low cost, and which I could adapt. I've written up some of these ideas in a short outline, and I wonder if you would like me to bring it over for you to review."

A smile crosses Nelson's face. He feels a growing excitement about what he could do with a person like Blue. His resistance caves in.

"That's a good suggestion, Rich, why don't you plan to come over on Friday. I'll clear my schedule in the afternoon, and we can go over this in more detail."

"OK, I'll plan to be there around 2:00 p.m."

"Great, and Rich?"

"Yes?"

"Why don't you ask your wife if she would like to join us later for dinner?"

Rich Blue played his end game masterfully. He proved to the potential employer that he was the best one for the job. Was he really? Perhaps another candidate would have worked out even better. No one will ever know. Or care. Rich made the move that got the job offer. His follow-up was not the typical "Have you decided who you are going to hire yet?" approach, it was an action based upon the communication of value, in answer to a possible negative.

More mileage can be gained by a well-timed, well-planned follow-up presentation than by perhaps any other single action in your work search. A good follow-up to an interview is a way of protecting your investment.

And it is not just for assistant city managers. A good follow-up work for secretaries, nurses, waiters, ranch foremen, consultants, and everyone else in the job game.

A good follow-up strategy will probably increase your odds of getting the job offer you want by 30%. Or more.

Please remember that interviewers are human. After they talk to six or seven candidates for a position, it all starts to get a bit hazy. When you recontact the employer, you consciously reinforce the favorable image you wish to project. You bump yourself ahead of other candidates in the interviewer's consciousness, by associating yourself directly with the solution to the employer's needs. And you accelerate the decision-making process, which is valuable whether the answer comes up positive or negative.

BLASTING OUT OF THE FILE DRAWER

There is a twofold purpose to your follow-up activities:

- To increase the likelihood of your receiving a job offer
- To accelerate the employer's decision

You will also find out how you stand and what stage the employer's decision-making process is in. Good follow-up is an art. It is based upon your personal acquaintance with the interviewer. Much of the initial "coldness" of the relationship is probably gone. You have also had the chance to learn more about what the employer does, how he or she has responded to your personal presentation, and what the job opportunity is about. In other words, better groundwork has been laid for communications between you and the employer. You can build on the relationship.

The most effective follow-up is initiated by telephone or, in the case of some of the more basic entry level positions, in person. Follow-up by mail is acceptable but generally less effective. The next step after the follow-up phone call might very well be another meeting, or a meeting with the next level of decision maker in the employment process. Or it could be a job offer.

The follow-up begins immediately after you have completed an interview. Before the experience fades into the murky past, within 30 minutes if possible, sit down with a note pad and answer the following questions in writing:

- Do you want to receive an offer from this employer? (Even if you don't, answer the balance of the questions.)
- What valuable things about yourself did you fail to communicate clearly enough?
- What questions would you like to have asked and didn't?
- What questions were asked of you which you feel you didn't answer clearly enough?
- What do you feel are the most positive impressions the employer got about you?
- What do you feel are the most negative impressions the employer got about you?
- Knowing what you now know about the job, what do you feel would be your strongest possible contribution?
- What information or attributes would you like to reinforce with the employer?
- How could you improve your personal presentation, either verbally or physically?
- What would be the next step to achieve with this employer (second interview, offer, etc.)?

TACTIC #74

List all of the points for post-interview follow-up on one sheet or card, with blank spaces to write in answers and responses. Make a number of photocopies of this for use after each interview.

COMPLETION CHECK ☐

Some of the specific things which you can accomplish with your follow-ups are these:

To remind the employer who you are
To provide the employer with specific information which you did not have available at the time of the interview
To clear up any confusion you might have left with the employer
To discover what the employer thinks of your ability to do the job
To change any mistaken impressions
To repeat and reinforce the positive information you conveyed
To ask the employer if he is considering you for the job, or planning to make you an offer.
To arrange for the next step to occur

TACTIC #75

If you have already had interviews when you are reading this, and for future interviews, mark your calendar five working days from the time of your last interview—note on a card what it is you feel would be most valuable for you to convey; remind yourself, in writing or in a role play, why you should be hired; and then communicate with each previous interviewer.

COMPLETION CHECK ☐

RECAPITULATE THE BENEFIT

You know by now that the way to get hired is to communicate such a clear sense of value to the potential employer that he is left with little question that you are the best person for the job.

The purpose of your follow-up is to reinforce or expand the employer's experience of your value.

The best way to accomplish this is to look for a new way to express or demonstrate value. You can refer back to something which came up during the interview and highlight how you could handle it:

> Miss Cox, this is Helen Starkes, we met last Thursday about Mrs. Popenoe's position. I'm the person who was working part-time for the Estuary Club, remember me?
> Good. I've been thinking about what you told me about wanting to reorganize the office, and the more I consider it, the more confident I am of my ability to make a contribution. You know, we had to do that twice at the club, and I supervised both reorganizations. I know that experience would be relevant. Do you think we could meet again so that I can show you the outline which I prepared?

Another way is to provide some additional information about a problem discussed. In other words, to start to contribute to the solution even before you get the job:

> Mr. Bellsey, this is Jan Burns, we met for a few moments last Friday afternoon while I was in your building. Remember? You mentioned to me that you were interested in having your training materials put on tape cassettes. I took the liberty of contacting two people I know who have done that, and they have recommended several sound studios and production houses. I'd like to stop by and give the names to you since it could be helpful. Will you be in this afternoon around 4:00 p.m.?

END GAME

You correct negative information, not by apologizing, but by adding offsetting advantages:

> Mr. Andrew, this is Peter Stiles. We had the pleasure of a brief interview last week on campus. You may not remember me, since I know you had a very full schedule that day. I was the person who talked about a fight with my art teacher. I wanted to call you to expand on that since I know it could have left an unfavorable impression. After our interview, as a result of what you said, I met with that teacher and apologized for my behavior. He and I spent over an hour together, and now I am back in the class on very friendly terms. So thank you for that suggestion. Since we didn't get around to discussing my design work, I've put together a collection of some of the things I've done which I'd like to show you next week. I think you'll find them to be relevant to your business.

It is not necessary for you to cook up a highly elaborate presentation to demonstrate the value which you can contribute. Nor are the details of what you can do what make the biggest difference. What is important is the *position* or purpose which you communicate. The very fact that you are interested in making a contribution and that you communicate that enthusiastically will often be as important as anything else.

TACTIC #76

Consider three basic human (nontechnical) attributes which you feel you possess. Write them down in sentence form in a way which you feel demonstrates how you would be a valuable asset to a potential employer. Communicate them out loud to a friend or a tape recorder. Sound convincing.

COMPLETION CHECK ☐

REMEDIAL ACTION

One of the major benefits of a well-thought-out follow-up campaign is that you can use it as an opportunity to correct any mistaken impressions, to patch up any holes in your presentation, and even to change an employer's mind about you.

Most candidates coming away from an interview, particularly one at which they don't feel they made their best impression, are reluctant to take action, and have the tendency to simply write off the experience and move on to the next interview. Don't. A good follow-up call, properly timed, can do quite a lot to change a faulty first impression, to supply missing information, even to elevate a person's chances from the reject pile to active consideration.

As we have said in our earlier tactic, after each interview review your performance and look for things which could have been communicated better or more clearly. Think of relevant accomplishments you could have described, or examples you could have given. Are there any questions that you wanted to ask and didn't?

Even if you are not sure that you want the position, go after it anyway. You can always turn down an offer if you are not interested in it. It will be good practice in testing your limits—how far you can go in turning a situation to your advantage.

TACTIC #77

Use this if you need a big push for a position you really want, but didn't do the most convincing job in the interview, and you haven't heard from them yet.

Have someone whose name you gave as a reference call the employer a week later, announce that she or he was one of the references given, and that, having been out for all or part of the week, your reference wanted to be sure that the employer hadn't tried to reach her or him and missed, and that the reference wanted to give an opinion of you as a worker.

COMPLETION CHECK ☐

THE NEW YOU

Frequently people come to our workshops, get to the part about résumés, and, as they slash out major areas of confusion and unconsciousness, complain about the fact that their junky old résumé is in the hands of a dozen or so employers—some of them interviewed with, some not. The problem is quickly turned to advantage when we explain to them that when they redo their résumé it will be a very natural time for them to visit or write the employer in order to exchange their brand-new résumé for the outdated one, and in the process to remind the employer of the contribution they can make.

If you use the mails, be sure to include a cover letter describing why the employer should be reminded of your abilities, and suggesting the next step, which may be another interview up the line, or an offer.

It is possible in the above tactic to prepare a brand-new résumé focused for a particular employer or skill. If you do so, don't make the mistake of sending the original. Make a few copies even if you don't need them, so the employer won't think that you are over-eager.

TRY ME

One of the more successful ways to break out of a logjam is to get the employer to use you on a trial basis. This can work wonders if the employer is undecided. Simply approach the employer with the following suggestion:

> I know that you are having a difficult time deciding who to hire for this position. Why don't we get together for 90 days, and you can try me on the job. If you aren't totally satisfied with the contribution I am making, then we can part company amicably. If you are pleased, as I am convinced you will be, we can continue on a more long-term relationship.

People will frequently take a bigger risk on a short-term basis than if they feel they are making a more permanent decision.

WHEN THE ANSWER IS NO

Don't stop with the first or second no from an employer. Get at least three before you are willing to give up. If you receive a turndown letter, call up, acknowledge the letter, don't argue that they made the wrong decision, simply tell them you know that there were things that you did not communicate clearly about yourself, which could possibly demonstrate how the employer would benefit from your affiliation. Suggest that you get together to review one more time.

This follow-up technique coming on top of a rejection has been used frequently by job seekers with surprisingly positive results.

Even if you don't turn the situation around, there are important secondary benefits you can obtain from any follow-ups you get.

- You may find out about new openings in other divisions.
- You can get the names of other employers or agencies in the field.

One of the most important things to watch out for is not getting stuck with trying to apologize for or explain the negatives. Don't add weight to negative information. Add additional advantages, rather than explain or justify the disadvantages.

WHEN THE ANSWER IS YES

The underlying truth in this book is that *you can make a difference in the quality of your worklife.* This is the single unquestioned observation we have made from our exposure to thousands of individual job seekers, and their use of the self-directed job search techniques we have shared with you.

By following these techniques you will be able to come up with interviews and offers in a career target field which will prove satisfying and expanding. Don't jump at the first offer as though your life depended upon it. Know that by following the techniques we have exposed you to, you can reactivate your job campaign at any level. If your job targets do not appear to be paying back with the kind of personal energy you expected, step back a few paces and rediscover them. If you are running out of employers to contact, dig in with some new sources of job market research information and get back on the phone. At every level in the job search you will find that there are additional steps for you to follow which will produce positive results for you. What you will discover is that *the final secret of the job search is your willingness to get what you want in life.* If you are willing, you will follow the tactics with ease. If you are unwilling, then each tactic will look like an obstacle rather than a way to gain control of a valuable life process.

The final measure of the job offers you receive is your own index of the satisfaction and aliveness which you will be able to experience in the day-by-day fulfillment of the work tasks which you perform, and the value and contribution you will make to others.

TACTIC #78

Do not accept the first offer you receive, unless you are certain that it is what you want. Set up a scale of five criteria which the ideal job would have. Measure each offer against this scale, and after you have scored the offers rank them in order of personal worth to you. You should have at least three possible offers before shutting off the flow of new potential, and accepting the one that gets you what you are looking for.

COMPLETION CHECK [ ]

GOODBYE

This is the end of the book for us, and the inauguration of a process for you. If you haven't done the tactics yet, please go back to tactic #1 on page 9, and start doing them.

Look back over your progress from time to time and see what tactics you have skipped, if any. Clean them up before moving on.

As you accomplish each tactic and step, please know that we are behind you, and that what you are doing will have a valuable lifetime payoff. Acknowledge yourself, as you go along, for the contribution you are making to your own life, and for the personal satisfaction and aliveness which it brings. And thank you for letting us participate with you in this process.

Q. Is this the end?

A. No. It's the beginning.